Hold on to your Dreams

Derrick B. Thomas

BLACKHEATH DAWN
PUBLISHING

Blackheath Dawn Publishing 2015

Blackheath Dawn Publishing
Hafren House.
Halesworth. Suffolk.
IP19 9HB, England

Email: info@blackheathdawn.co.uk

Hold on to Your Dreams

ISBN 978-1-911368-08-3
This is a third impression and carries revisions

Previously published August 2014 in an edition edited by Multimedia Reputations

For more information on the author,
enquiries@blackheathdawn.co.uk

Foreword

I was introduced to Derrick in 1996 by a very good friend of mine who had met him at an exhibition for black businesses. He was just into his sixtieth year then, but looked twenty years younger. I was impressed by his energy and enthusiasm, but fundamentally his optimism. He was always positive: nothing phased him. Even as a youth, Derrick had been ceaselessly forward looking. He travelled extensively throughout his career, and remained focused on the goals that he set for himself.

When he talked about his life and experiences, I wondered what it was that made him different to all the other young black men that came to Britain in the 1950's and 1960's. I concluded it was simply a desire to succeed and a refusal to allow outward forces, such as other people's prejudices, to dictate how his life would turn out.

Derrick Bobbington Thomas is an example of what is possible, as long as you have faith, determination and a positive outlook.

June Hamilton

Preface

I grew up in Guyana and unlike many, was lucky to have comfortable life. I was certainly stubborn but also fortunate and determined, so much so that I was able to enjoy a successful life. That does not and never did, blind me to the people of this world that struggle to survive.

The 'Third world' as it was known, had so many young people faced with a lifetime of struggle and poverty. They did almost anything, legal or illegal just to survive.

I am an African Caribbean and moved to the UK late 1950's. I saw at first hand the problems that many of my compatriots were experiencing as they tried to find work and a place to live in a land that was far from welcoming.

Today, sadly, in many parts of the world, too may young people are still born into dreadful poverty to fasce the same uphill struggle for survival. There difficulties are exacerbated by their lack of education. Lack of life chances and often in the face of prejudices

I hope that my story and its title, will inspire and encourage all who come across it, to never give up on their dreams and to seize lifes chances come what may.

Derrick B. Thomas (2014)

Contents

Chapter 1

A TRUE SON of McKENZIE

I remember I always used to get into trouble for being too inquisitive. During our summer holidays we used to go to relatives who lived across the river on the West Bank of Demerara. On the occasion of one visit, they had just finished building an outdoor toilet about 50 yards or so away from the house. I wanted to be the first one to use this toilet; so as soon as the carpenter put the last nail in the door I decided I was going to use it. Like all the boys, I wore short trousers and had a habit of not putting the buckle through the belt loops, consequently when I undid my trousers in the new toilet building, my belt fell down the hole. "It's a new toilet," I thought and when I looked down the hole I saw the belt in what I thought looked like shallow water. I noticed a piece of wood inside the hole, and thought that if I balanced on the wood and stretched down the hole I would be able to reach my belt. Unfortunately the 'wood' was mud; I slipped and fell into the hole. I had water up to my knees, mosquitoes were everywhere. It was a nightmare! Of course I panicked. I shouted for help, but nobody heard me. It was getting dark. I must have been in there for at least two hours. (In the interim I retrieved my belt) At last I heard my cousin's voice. I shouted so loudly as was about to enter the new toilet, she was very startled. She rushed to tell my father and uncle and they came running each carrying their deer hunting double-barrelled shot gun, with torch lights strapped to the barrels. They burst in and pointed their guns at me. I shouted 'No Daddy, it's me!' They pulled me outside and my mother beat me for another two hours, hosed me down from head to toe and scrubbed me till I thought my skin was going to come off – all for being nosey.

I was born in Guyana on October 15th 1936. My father was a General Foreman of the exploration party for Demerara Bauxite Company, which had mined bauxite for around a hundred years in Guyana at that time. My mother was a teacher who, like many of her contemporaries, stopped working and dedicated her time to looking after the household and bringing up their children. My mother's great passion for education remained throughout her life, and she passed this passion on to her children.

Mum, Adele who must be obeyed

Our family enjoyed a very good standard of living in Guyana. In the town of McKenzie where I was born, workers were paid the highest salaries in the West Indies. Consequently many people travelled there from Jamaica, Grenada, St. Vincent, St. Lucia and Barbados to work for the Bauxite Company. During the Second World War, bauxite became very important for making aluminium and various other products. Ships came from faraway places such as Norway, Sweden, Canada, U.S.A. and England to carry the bauxite all over the world. So even from this small Guyanese community, as a young man, I gained a vision of a far wider world.

One of my childhood friends, Leslie Hubbert, recalled that the environment in McKenzie was one of safety, where children were protected and received encouragement. Parents were, on the whole, ambitious for their children; and the wider community equally applauded the individual achievement of individuals. So for me, growing up in Guyana was great! My life was filled with outdoor activities provided by the rich green forests and being a Boy Scout, I had regular opportunities for camping. At school I played sports such as cricket and football; and even as a young schoolboy, I was disciplined enough to get up at 5.30 in the morning to go to athletics training sessions.

I was fortunate enough to have a community pool directly behind my house so I learned to swim at a very early age.

Leon Quamina, another childhood friend, remembers me as being very advanced for my years. Even though I was two years older than Leon, appar-

McKenzie Primary School. 1940-1977

ently I still seemed to him to be precociously driven, determined to meet challenges and complete tasks.

Mischief

I was still a boy and, like so many young boys, I was a prankster and used to get up to all sorts of tricks. My mother used to call me 'That bad man from Brimstone.'

As a choirboy in St. Aiden's church in Wismar, I attended church three times each Sunday: Sunday morning for Morning service, Sunday school and Evensong. Since we frequently misbehaved my friends and I were often refused entry onto the boat that took us across the Demerara River to church. We would plead with the boatman to let us ride, eventually wearing him down so much that he would agree. Then we would repay him by stealing his jacket and lantern and burying them!

During one Carol Service I stuck a pin in the baritone's bottom while he was singing Hark the Herald Angels Sing. For this I received a good beating from the priest in the vicarage.

Then there was the time when I wrapped pieces of soap in toffee paper to give to my friends at school. It would have been a great trick, were it not for my mother finding them in my trouser pocket and sharing them between my brothers and sisters. I got a beating for that too!

So truly, as a lad, I was very 'naughty.'

But there was also a side to me that was serious and looked to the future. My friend, Leslie, said that I was so determined and tenacious there was never any doubt that an idea or dream of mine would one day become a reality.

It wasn't only about money and career, but also in terms of health and well-being. At the age of 13, with the aid of four friends, I started a body building club. Men like Steve Reeves, Charles Atlas and Rex Barker were our heroes, Icons from the muscle magazines we read so avidly. So we decided to start our own gym.

Of course, we couldn't afford to buy real weights, but we were resourceful boys and managed to make our own weights by using old wheels from disused carriages that we found at the railway yard. We used pipes for bars.. It was very dangerous because the weights would slide down the bars, since they weren't fixed in any way.

Walter 'Mosquito Physique' Jordan

We persisted, my friend's brother, seeing how serious we were, helped us by making some proper weights. We had very strict rules in this club. Two of the most important ones were no smoking and no drinking – a practice I've carried throughout my life. So between the ages of 13 and 19 years I was a bodybuilder and developed a very strong, muscular physique – even if I do say so myself!

Another of my friends, Walter Jordan, we nicknamed 'Mosquito Physique' because he was so thin. When he took his shirt off you could count his ribs. After four years of bodybuilding he won the title of 'Mr. BodyBuilder, Guyana.'

I acknowledged the importance of exercise from a very early age and my bodybuilding club was the beginning of a lifelong habit of regular exercise.

Whenever and wherever I travel the first things to go into my suitcase are my tracksuit and running shoes. I've run along the Bosphoros in Turkey; through deserts in Jordan and Dubai; along the banks of the Blue Danube; in the streets of Lagos, Nigeria; and in many other countries.

§ § § § §

My school was very good to me and I had two brothers and two sisters. We had a wonderful social and family life. My mother, Adele, was the disciplinarian in the family. She controlled everything. My father, James, used to bring in his wages at the end of each week and put it straight into mum's hands. As a young boy I disapproved of this and always vowed that I would never let any woman take my money.

My father had complete, unquestioning trust in my mother and as far as I could gather, she always gave him all the money he wanted, but she certainly controlled the purse strings!

My father was a very kind man, despite his deep, loud voice and although in Guyana at that time it was an acceptable form of discipline, he never beat his children. One disapproving look was enough to establish order in his house. My mother did all the necessary beating, as well as solving any other problems which arose in the Thomas household. Her strictness was tempered by her love of music and poetry.

I remember the Christmas that was my brother's 21st birthday. He decided to go drinking with his friends to celebrate. On his way back home he was struggling across the road when my mother saw him coming.

She sat in her rocking chair and asked me whether he looked like he was drunk. To get him into trouble I said 'Yes.' The rocking chair went faster and faster.

My brother went into the kitchen but stumbled on the sill and vomited. That was the last straw! My mother came into the kitchen and hit him so hard that he was sobered up immediately and that was the last time he returned home drunk!

My mother loved to watch me teaching my sister how to dance to the strains of Victor Sylvester or Joe Loss from the radio. Mrs.Thomas placed great emphasis on manners. She was fond of using the cliché 'Manners maketh the man' and used to tell us no matter how much education we had, good manners were more important, although it was preferable to have both.

I certainly benefited from a good early education, as well as a very loving, supportive and disciplined family environment.

I attended the Government School in McKenzie with my brothers and sisters. At that time the school was run by the Canadian Company that mined the bauxite. The school was one of the best in the Caribbean. Offering a very high standard of education. Teachers from other islands often visited to observe its good practice. Even though the two other communities around McKenzie – Wismar and Christiansburg – had their own schools, because of its reputation some children still crossed the river to attend the McKenzie school.

My eldest brother, Cecil, was four years my senior and did his apprenticeship as a welder in McKenzie with the Bauxite Company. We got on well. Cecil was more homely than I was and, unlike me, he didn't play much sport. In a way my parents wished that I was more like my older brother, but clearly I was quite the opposite, much bolder.

I had one younger brother, Mackie, and two sisters, Joy and Barbara. Joy and I were, perhaps, the closest because we were both born in October. We did things together that we didn't do with the others.

I did not get to know my younger brother very well, because I left McKenzie when he was still a teenager. But Mackie did come to England in the 1960's and we managed to form quite a close relationship. Mackie became an engineer at the Post Office and he studied for his Master's degree in Computer and Business Studies in England.

He went back to Guyana in 1996 and taught Business Studies and Computer Science at the University of Guyana until his retirement when he returned to the U.K.

My younger sister, Barbara, became a school teacher at the McKenzie School before she eventually left Guyana and Joy, the older girl, became a nurse. Unfortunately, Joy died of cancer in 1988. It was a sad time for all the family and even though she was younger than me, I felt I had lost a mother as well as a sister. She was the one who kept in contact with any one that we had ever known from Guyana; old school friends, long lost family and anyone else we knew from home. She was a very friendly, open and kind woman. A great loss to the family.

§ § § § §

It is clear that our mother's background in education played a very important part in the Thomas children's lives, and the family was very successful indeed in terms of their chosen careers.

My education continued until 1953 when, at the age of seventeen years, armed with my School Certificate and Woodworking Certificate, I began work as an Assistant Trainee Manager for a large department store. I was sent there with a school friend to be trained in management. Although I enjoyed the training, it became clear to me that this was not what I wanted to do.

I had two main ambitions. One was to become a marine engineer, and the other was to serve an apprenticeship in the company where my father worked. The Demerara Bauxite Company had no vacancies for motor engineers at that time; neither could I find an apprenticeship in marine engineering. I stayed at the department store for about a year before making the decision to move on.

In 1955 I decided to leave my family and McKenzie and go to the capital, Georgetown, which according to Sam Blackett, who grew up with me in McKenzie, was a very bold and unusual step.

He said of me 'As a mid-teenager he displayed the strength of character of a person who already knew what he wanted in life and was determined to achieve his goal. His journey started when he left home to start an apprenticeship in the city.'

Some years later Sam and I were reunited in England and Sam was not surprised to see me still finding challenges to add to my achievements.

§ § § § §

I lived in Georgetown with my uncle, Bertie Daniels, who was a captain for Bookers Coastal Shipping. An incredibly flamboyant character, Bertie subsequently changed his name to Bertie Lochinvar, a name he felt was more suited to his personality.

Bertie Lochinvar's job was to take cargo from Guyana to Trinidad and from there to Barbados and Jamaica. Sometimes he would be away at sea for two or three months at a time. He lost his right hand when the glove he was wearing got caught in a winch on a schooner. I thought he was a great captain and I loved and admired him very much.

Every school holiday I used to travel with him. I remember a time when I was about 13 years old, we were caught in a hurricane between Guyana and Trinidad. We left Guyana about eight o'clock at night. The moon and stars were bright and the sea was so calm. We were chatting, you know, making seamen jokes. Suddenly the wind roared, the sky became dark, and the waves crashed. The boat began to rock. Immediately my uncle roared 'Batten down the hatches!' Everyone ran to their posts and tied down everything that moved. Within ten minutes a huge storm hit us; I thought I would never see my mother again. The boat was lifted twenty to thirty feet in the air by the waves, and then dropped down into what appeared to be a deep black hole. We hit the bottom and came back up again.

This is how ships have disappeared without any trace. Simple as that! .... Just as suddenly the storm abated, the sea became calm. The moon came out from behind the clouds, it was as if nothing had happened! It is an experience I will never forget. I was really impressed with my uncle's command of his ship and of his men that night.

Captain Bertie Lochinvar,Bookers Coastal shipping, Guyana.

Years later, in 1996 I had a vivid reminder of this incident with my Uncle. I attended the Southampton Boat Show with a colleague from Allied Dunbar. This colleague had a brokerage selling yachts and sailing accessories. We finished on a Sunday afternoon and had to sail this yacht which, ironically, was called Good Luck, back to Ipswich. At about six o'clock we left Southampton. While we were sailing around the Brighton coast up to Hastings there was a huge storm, gale force 8. We were in a 35-foot yacht but it was like being in a bubble in the air. We couldn't come into shore because it was very rocky around the area.

It brought back memories of Uncle Bertie and what had happened to me when I was thirteen years old.

The yacht behind us ran aground and two people drowned that same day just off the Brighton Coast. We sailed out to sea and were sailing through the shipping lanes and we had to dodge the big liners; it was like a nightmare.

Only three of us were on that boat, two men and a woman who was a nurse. She was a very calm person; but she could not get around the deck as nimbly as I could, so I was the one running around the side of the deck. To make certain that he would not be swept away we tied the captain to the steering wheel and I fed him with coffee and sandwiches. Luckily I didn't get seasick! After the storm we found ourselves off the coast of France. We could see the French coastal beacons. The following morning we set sail back to England. We put into Hastings and we never made it to Ipswich. My friend found someone to help him crew the boat back to Ipswich. We were lucky and so fortunate. One yacht, which was trying to get into Brighton, hit rocks because of that same storm. We saw its lights but suddenly it disappeared. We heard what had happened on a news bulletin that reported the captain as being very competent and was quoted as saying 'we're not going into shore, let's go out to sea and ride out the storm there.' Our decision to go into the shipping lanes where if anything happened we were more likely to be spotted and picked up proved absolutely correct in this instance. It was all good experience. Great times. Great weekend. We were the fortunate and lucky people.

My Uncle Bertie played a very influential role in my life in many ways; I even found the way he dressed impressive. A great lover of English style, Bertie Lochinvar would import most of his clothes from England. He wore spats over his shoes and double-breasted jackets with gold chains. Every suit had a hat and shoes to match it. I used to love to see him all dressed up, particularly when he was wearing his uniform. Not surprisingly then some of his style rubbed off on me. He was a well liked and well respected figure, and even today, when I return to Guyana for holidays, people still remember my uncle Bertie Lochinvar.

Although there were aspects of my uncle's character I didn't approve of; for example, his wife's sister used to live in the flat below where we were living and her husband was also working on the same ship with my uncle. However, she also had a boyfriend and my uncle heard about it. He became afraid his own wife would do the same, so he would regularly interrogate me about my aunt. It was very uncomfortable as a seventeen year old to be put into that position.

However, I liked the fact that he was a great disciplinarian and as with my mother, education featured very highly on Bertie Lochinvar's agenda. Uncle Bertie encouraged me to enrol at the Government Technical Institute and also to take private lessons in Junior and Senior Cambridge examinations. So twice a week I attended college for my apprenticeship and studied for my Cambridge examination as well as doing my apprenticeship. My young life was packed and already showing signs of an active go-getter.

§ § § § §

My friend Oswald and I each found a job in a motor car repair shop in a place called Robb Street. I vividly remember Mr. Gooding at Robb Street paying 35cents for a week's work. That would buy a milk shake and lovely Guyanese bread called Tennis Rolls.

When I first saw the money in his hand I thought Mr. Gooding wanted me to run an errand to buy something, not that he was in fact giving me my wages! Seeing the look on my face, Mr. Gooding said, 'Son, don't worry. You take it from me, if you learn your job to the best of your ability; money will be no problem for you. You will earn much more than that. This is what you are here for, not for the pay!' Despite the disappointment, I took the advice and indeed, my pay did keep rising regularly. I stayed with Mr. Gooding for around six months until the Rootes Group in Guyana accepted me into an apprenticeship.

Working with Rootes Group was something I had always been very interested in. I'd always enjoyed working with engines and cars. As a young boy I used to love pulling things apart, even though I was not always able to put them back together! I was a very inquisitive young man, always wanting to know how things worked. Under the wing of Claude Fraser in my apprenticeship, I worked on many different cars, pulling them apart and, fortunately, learning how to put them back together again. I studied for my City & Guilds at the Technical Institute in Guyana and privately for my Junior and Senior Cambridge examinations.

Just before I was due to leave Rootes Group Guyana, to join Rootes in England, my English manager in Guyana called me in his office to give me my papers before I left and I had a little lecture.

'You will find in England most English men go to work in pinstripe suits and bowler hats.'

Surprise! Surprise! When I arrived at the workshop I found the workshop floor was cleaned by an Englishman wearing a dirty overcoat.

A last trip on the steam ship R H Carr before Leaving Guyana in 1957

CHAPTER 2

LIFE'S TRAVELS BEGIN.

At around twenty years of age my parents encouraged me to travel. At the time, many people were emigrating, their destinations America, Canada and England. My father had travelled, to Jamaica, where he spent eighteen months teaching the employees at the bauxite mine how to use a special diamond drill. My mother, never having the opportunity to travel herself, felt that it was important for me to do so. She saw it as an opportunity for me to develop and of the family, with the exception of my uncle; I was the only one to show any interest at all in travelling.

At that time I was torn, I loved the freedom and beauty of Guyana. I decided, however, to go with the intention of getting a good education, and returning after five years, the period away that was often quoted by many in those days of mass emmigration and hope. I cried and cried when my mother booked my passage. The prospect of leaving Georgetown was a very sad one, but I decided to take the opportunity and in June 1957 I left Guyana. I spent about a month in Trinidad with my Uncle, travelling and touring the Island, before I eventually left the Caribbean in July 1957. My parents never travelled and by the time I could afford to bring them over, sadly both of them had died. The rest of my family remains in Guyana to this day, apart from my sister, Barbara, in the USA. and my brother, Mackie, who now lives in the UK.

The voyage from Trinidad on the Italian liner TV Venezuela took me and my fellow passengers to many countries, for example Barbados and Tenerife, where I remember clearly the striking image of blue-eyed, blond butcher women chopping up meat and selling it in a market. We also stopped in Barcelona, Las Palmas and Florence before travelling for two days by train from Florence via Rome, through Paris and down to Calais.

During my stay in Florence I was followed around by a man who kept asking where my tail was. My first experience of racism.

We eventually disembarked at Victoria Station, London, on 1st August 1957

NATIONAL SERVICE – encounters with prejudice

The large brown envelope came through the post. I opened it and saw 'You have completed two years in the United Kingdom and are now eligible to be conscripted for National Service.... and so on.' Most black people were enlisted into the Army or the RAF regiment to do guard duty. I thought 'I don't want to go in the Army. Eitherof the other forces – the Navy, the Air Force;but not the Army.'

It was April 1959 I was called up for National Service which was a compulsory two year period. All young men resident in the UK had to serve in the armed forces and somehow, even though I knew about it, I didn't expect it. In fact I was one of the last young men to be called up in 1959 and national service conscription was abolished later that same year.

I was working with the Rootes Group at the time, and my friends tried to persuade me to go to France for six months thinking that by the time I came back the authorities would have forgotten about me!

Luckily, I ignored their advice and instead took it as an opportunity to do something different. Straightaway I decided that I wanted to go into the Air Force. I had just finished my City & Guilds in Motor Vehicles at Paddington Polytechnic and, equipped with these qualifications, I believed I was RAF material.

I arrived at the Recruitment Office in Ealing, gave my papers to the recruitment officer who was about the same age as myself. He assumed that I would be going into the Army, and when I said that I was not, the young man asked, rather condescendingly, 'Can you pass the test for the RAF?'

'Well, try me!' I said.

The mental arithmetic and non-verbal reasoning tests caused me no problems whatsoever and I astonished the recruitment officer with the speed with which I completed them. I responded to the young man's surprised expression by telling him that he had completely the wrong idea about black people. 'I may even have more qualifications than you!' I said.

Derrick and his apprentice 1959

My test was successful and I was admitted into the Royal Air Force. I also had to complete the trade test for the motor department of the air force based at RAF Wilmslow, near Blackpool, which was the motor department for the Air Force and was subsequently posted to RAF Northwood in Middlesex, where I spent about eight months.

Around two years after I had joined I found out that the level at which I had passed the tests did not get me the corresponding rank. I had passed at the Junior Technician rank and all I was given was AC1, a much lower grade, the result no doubt of prejudice. It was unusual for a black man to join the RAF, let alone enter at such a high rank. The men under his command would not stand for it! Or so it was assumed.

I remember that the night before I took the exam there was another airman who had previously left the Air Force and was coming back. He had told me that he was terrified of the exam and out of kindness I took him through the old paper. He was made a Corporal after the test. But this didn't mean much to me at the time. I'd got what he wanted – to be in the Air Force. It was only on reflection, after two years in the service, that I realised what had happened. I didn't do anything about it because there was nothing I could do at the time. Many other incidents of racism and prejudice were to follow. This was the first. But somehow they only seemed to strengthen my resolve.

§ § § § §

Not a man who was willing to allow the grass to grow under my feet, it was not long before I decided I wanted to change my trade. This didn't surprise my commanding officer in the least. When I approached my Flight Sergeant in the motor department he had already been observing me and had apparently realised over time that I was not suited for the motor department. He was impressed by the way I carried myself and by the way I spoke.

He noticed that I was meticulous about my appearance. I would change out of my overalls after work. My uniform was always pressed, clean and pristine. He even noticed that I had special work boots, which I changed after my shift was over. Flight Sergeant Dwyer had no hesitation in putting me forward to another trade and he told me he would 'sign any papers' that were necessary.

I wanted to go on missiles, but Dwyer suggested I go for navigational instruments or aircraft electrical and electronics. I took Dwyer's advice and chose electrics. I had to take another test, plus an eye test, which I passed effortlessly, and was posted to RAF Melksham based in Wiltshire, where I qualified as an aircraft electrical fitter. I have been eternally grateful to Flight Sergeant Dwyer for giving me that first opportunity which led to so many other things.

RAF Melksham was a training camp so there was a constant flow of people who came in to be trained, and then they'd leave. I was the only black perma-

First posting, RAF Melksham

nent staff member there. All the others were white. This didn't stop me, however, from becoming chairman for the airmen's club or making friends with my commanding officer whose name was Group Captain Davies. For some reason he took a liking to me. He had a nickname for me, 'Thomas Boy.' Nowadays many black men would see that as a typical historical racist insult but in Group Captain Davies it may not have been as he had a Welsh name although I don't know whether he was actually Welsh but 'boy' is a common term there used in the same way as 'mate' etc.

Certainly, despite his rank, he didn't appear to think he was superior. He would always salute his men before they saluted him and was the first commander I ever came across who used to serve breakfast to his men!

Group Captain Davies was a great disciplinarian, and everybody on the camp was afraid of him, but he and I got on very well, perhaps because he saw in me a kindred spirit – another disciplined person. In the evenings, as a trained motor mechanic and always alert to opportunities, I used to repair the cars of some of the other airmen and officers. I used my skills to make some extra money to visit friends and family in London. In the evenings Group Captain Davies walked his dog past my billet and we used to talk about his way up through the ranks. We became very good friends.

My wish to rise to challenges enabled me to gain accelerated promotion. Usually it would take three years to rise from Junior Technician to Corporal, but because of a fortuitous incident I was rewarded. My unit used to put on an exhibition every year and that year it was in Glasgow, commemorating the Battle of Britain and navigational instruments were all displayed and explained by the navigational engineers. Before the exhibition opened one of the sergeants who was in charge of navigational instruments became ill and the Flying Officer at the time FO Niles, asked me to take his place. Regardless of my protestations that I was an electronic engineer who knew little about navigational instruments, Niles said all I needed was 'A quick run-down of what I was supposed to do and I would be fine.' I eventually agreed and learned about the instruments from Niles the night before.

The day the exhibition opened, dressed in a white coat, looking as sharp as a razor and very scientific, I went through the operation of all the navigational instruments to the twenty people at the stand. Meanwhile Niles stood back and watched the young, nervous Junior Technician eventually fall into the flow of the exhibition and because I knew what I was talking about, grow in confidence.

When I finished Niles approached me and told me I had done a brilliant job. Thirteen people were recruited that day due to my demonstrations. Niles joked that I should be transferred to the recruitment area! When we returned to Melksham it was because of Niles' favourable report of my performance that I received accelerated promotion.

§ § § § §

Glasgow Battle of Britain exhibition

In our lives sometimes opportunities present themselves but we don't always take them. However, I was a man who grasped each opportunity that came up. One day I was working in a hanger and I was singing 'When I fall in love.' The Station Technical Officer came up quietly behind me and said 'Seems like you are enjoying your work. How would you like to go on flight simulators?' I was hesitant at first but only because I didn't know exactly what a flight simulator was.

In those days they had what they called link trainers. These were older versions of what we now know as flight simulators. These were used, as their name implies, to train the pilots to fly. Even though I had admitted that I knew very little about flight simulators the Technical Officer was undeterred. Again, my punctuality, hard work and dedication had impressed my superiors. The Technical Officer promised to send me on a course at RAF Lynham in Wiltshire. The only thing that worried me was my lack of knowledge, so I was sent away for a month's training at RAF Lynham, working on the Comet and Britannia Aircraft simulators to see how I got along with the people and the technology. After the month was up, I decided I definitely would like the transfer, and five months later I was part of a team of twelve men sent to General Precision Systems in Aylesbury – a civilian company that built the Lightning flight simulator for the Air Force.

As was normal protocol, my background was investigated by MI6 before I was allowed to begin my new post in Aylesbury. After all I would be working on the most top secret aircraft in the air force at the time. This was the Lightning Simulator Mark VI Fighter aircraft, the first aircraft to fly above the speed of sound.

By this time I had become accustomed to being the only black man, or one of the very few, amongst my peers. But when I arrived at the factory in Aylesbury nobody except the men on my team, and my instructor, spoke to me. I would say good morning and good afternoon but no-one ever responded. This went on for about a month. Every day I greeted my colleagues. Every day I received silence until, suddenly one day, my persistence paid off.

One morning I said good morning to this woman and she said good morning back to me. Surprise! That was the beginning. From that moment, everybody else started. I'm one of these people believe that if you don't speak to me because I'm black it is you that has a problem, not me! I think because they had never had a black person working in that situation before they probably didn't know how to approach me. They needed someone to break the ice. I didn't have to work with anyone on the factory floor so it didn't matter. But once that happened, the floodgates opened. I was invited out to lunch in the canteen, everyone wanted to buy me lunch, wanted me to play on their darts teams. I became a mascot after that! I was invited to the mayor's ball at the local town hall, weekends here and there. I never questioned it, I just thought English people were very strange in their attitude. Even up to now it hasn't changed in some areas. I've been here for almost sixty years and you still get this sort of thing happening in certain areas. But I let it roll on …

§ § § § §

I never took my good fortune for granted. I was aware of the plight of many young black servicemen who fell foul of prejudice, or who were not lucky enough to have open-minded, observant commanding officers. But I was clear in my mind what my goals were. I was in the Royal Air Force for a particular time and a particular reason. I intended to get all the qualifications I could before I left the Air Force – whatever it took – so if they asked me to clean my badge twenty-five times a day, press my trousers and make my bed, I did it because I had a long-term goal, and that was just a step towards it.

I was fully aware that as a young man in my early twenties, no company in England would have taken me on as an apprentice at twenty-three years of age. Black people never worked with aircraft; it was written, and so made sure I gained as many qualifications, and as much training as I could. On other stations many men had a lot of problems when they tried to go to night school. They were prevented from doing so because they were deliberately put on shifts and they couldn't get day release. But I did manage to get day release, and other training, from day one. I never gave weight to the problems I had in the Air Force because of prejudice. In any case, I was shrewd enough to know that even in those days, it was against the rules to be openly racist in the Air Force, you could be court martialled for it. But, of course, it was done covertly.

I first met George Lawrence, another airman from Jamaica, at RAF Melksham when he was fresh out of basic training and eager to become an aircraft technician. He said I'd made life much easier for him and the handful of other Caribbean airmen and consequently we formed a bond that was to last for the rest of our lives. We later met again when he returned to advanced training. We were completing the same course and we became good friends. Lawrence said that overt racism was not as widespread in the Air Force as it was in civilian life. It was there, nevertheless, in people's attitudes, possibly because of ignorance.

However, Lawrence knew I was determined to make the most of the opportunities afforded me and he witnessed as I eventually became a highly skilled and qualified Simulator Service Engineer, one of the most competitive positions available to technical personnel.

The Station Commander and the Technical Officer, who was the highest technical rank on the station, always supported me so things generally ran smoothly for me. Nevertheless it would be unfair to underestimate my whole attitude, philosophy and approach to life. I firmly believed then, and still do now, that those doors were open to me because I was able to overlook the sometimes negative behaviour of others, was always committed to my work, and focused on my goals.

A lot of people were unable to take the humiliation and inequality that comes with prejudice. They had many problems in the Air Force. Some had to leave and some were put on charge. But for me, for most of the twelve years I spent in the Air Force, there were only a few small incidents which I was able to shrug off, I never really had any major problems. The one potentially explosive incident I recall was dealt with promptly and decisively by my commanding officer.

I was the highest rank in the entry on my fitter's course and during the evenings we were to clean our billets, make our beds, polish the floor and things like that. I asked one of the men under my supervision to carry out a duty which the Corporal had requested. He responded by saying 'Why are you black b.....d giving me orders?' I think people didn't like the fact that I was of a higher rank – they were probably jealous. I asked him to repeat what he said and he stormed out. Now, some black guys would have thumped him, but I went straight to my Squadron Leader, who in turn stormed out of his office and called the man in question to his office.

He said to him 'I want you to apologise to Senior Air Craft man Thomas for what you said, if not you'll be charged and discharged from the Air Force immediately' and he apologised to me. Squadron Leader Summers added 'If ever again you do anything like that – just whisper the word – and you're out on your neck! This Airman is twice the man you are!' From that day nothing like this ever happened again. It happened that once, and it was nipped in the bud straightaway.'

Never allowing words to hurt me, I would instead try to find a way to overcome them, like persistently saying good morning or strictly following orders. I used to say 'You guys can talk as much as you like but don't touch. When you touch me, then you are asking for problems, but you can do what you want to do as long as you don't touch me.'

The world outside the Air Force was quite different, however, and I recall vividly a disturbing incident that occurred while I was on weekend leave.

I had a flat in Ladbroke Grove. We used to arrive by coach to White City Stadium, the coach would leave us there, and we went to our various homes. One Sunday which was our usual night for returning to camp, I was going down to Latymer Road Station at 10.30 at night when the pubs were just closing down. Suddenly all these white people, men and women, came out. As soon as I got abreast of them they started on me, pelting me with stones and chains, and chasing me. There must have been about twenty of them. I was an athlete so I ran as fast as I could and I left them standing. They couldn't keep up with me. I ran to Shepherds Bush Station where eventually I saw a couple of policemen and I told them what had happened. They went away and came back after about fifteen minutes and said they hadn't seen anybody. I don't know how far twenty young men could have got in that time, but they said the people were gone.

In January 1960 it was in the local paper though. The Ladbroke Grove or Shepherds Bush paper, I can't remember which. When I got back to camp in the small hours of the morning I was so frustrated. I was so tense. I was trembling. I looked at all those guys sleeping; it was about 4 o'clock in the morning. I looked at the racks where we stored all the guns and considered. That was what I felt inside. From London to Melksham – I felt that tension all the way up there. That was the first time I felt like doing anybody any harm, but then the guys said 'Let's go back and find them – next weekend.' I didn't know who those guys were so there was no hope of finding them, but at least I felt the airmen were friends and on my side.

That was the nearest I ever actually came to any physical harm because of my race, even in the late 1950's when racial attacks, mostly carried out by Teddy Boys were rife, and particularly in the Ladbroke Grove area.

I remember stories I told to my sister who'd just come from Guyana. People used to pass by black people's houses and throw stones, breaking their windows. She had neither seen nor expected anything like this, and was petrified. In fact, as George Lawrence said 'Most of us were naïve to the bigotry in British society at first and had a rude awakening when faced with discrimination in jobs, housing etc.'

I considered myself very fortunate in a lot of ways to have come this far without experiencing such persistent abuse. There were the everyday incidents which black people had to face, of course. I remember once trying to get a room for a friend. I'd thought that if I dressed in my Air Force uniform and asked for this room, I would get it. When I knocked on the door and enquired about the room the landlady said it was taken and slammed the door in my face. Not willing to let the matter slide, I rang the number about half an hour later and, of course, because of my very clear voice and accent, people thought I was English.

The voice on the other end told me that the room was still vacant. Unfortunately this was a common tale told by many immigrants from the Caribbean and other parts of the Commonwealth at that time.

I met a lot of people and made a lot of friends during my fifteen month stay at General Precision Systems. I finished the course in 1966 and from there I was posted to Singapore for two and a half years. While I was in Singapore, I also spent time in Malaysia. I was surprised to find that there were a lot of black servicemen in Singapore, though most of them were in the Army. As almost happened to me, blacks tended to be pushed into the Army when they were called up for National Service, even if they tried to join the Air Force. But there were many black servicemen in the RAF Regiment. Their function was mostly keeping guard, parading, manning gun units, working as medical orderlies or in administration. Yet, in the technical jobs there were very few blacks. I was the only one on flight simulators in the Air Force probably during the whole twelve years I was there. Even now when I tell people I was in flight simulation, they are really surprised. The Air Force and the Navy were the preserve of the top people. You had to be well educated to join and obviously, quite mistakenly, it was thought that most black people were not eligible.

Life in Singapore was very easy! I had realised early on that playing sport was definitely an asset! They used to work about one hundred and sixty-five days a year. The rest of the time was holiday, mostly playing some kind of sport. There was no prejudice there. In fact, they seemed to like the blacks more. They liked the music. There were a lot of Jamaican airmen there and so reggae and calypso became very popular. Because of this I was taken on a social roller coaster of parties, weekend invitations and sports. I played Hockey, Badminton, Squash, Cricket and Football. Life in Singapore was special. I was invited everywhere.

I soaked up the different cultures that surrounded me and used it as an opportunity to learn about different people and traditions. I went to Sikh weddings, Chinese weddings, Malaysian weddings and lots of other functions which allowed me to experience the lives of different people. Playing sports also helped me to meet and mix with all sorts of different nationalities. To me it was not unlike the West Indies. You could get all the tropical foods and the weather was good. Apart from Indians and Chinese there were South Africans, Australians and New Zealanders and, best of all, they all played cricket together!

Sport in the forces certainly opened many doors for me and sometimes even enabled me to get out of normal duty. Once I was picked by the Squadron Leader who organised the cricket matches to play in the Far East Championship. The tour was to last for two weeks. When I informed his Flight Sergeant (my boss at the time) that the Squadron Leader wanted me on the team, he refused me permission to go. So, naturally, I had to inform the Squadron Leader who was not very happy about it.

'What?!' he said. 'Who told you that?'

I said 'My Flight Sergeant says I have to work.'

RAF Tengah 1966

He said 'You mean to tell me that with all the people in his section, he cannot allow you to go to play cricket for the camp?'

I said 'Those were his words.'

With that the Squadron Leader left and shot up to the flight simulator building.

'Flight Sergeant' he said. 'What is this I've heard that Derrick is not allowed to join the team?'

He said to the Squadron Leader 'No. He has to work.'

'You mean to tell me' he replied, 'That if he leaves here the whole simulator building is going to close down for two weeks?'

'Well, other people have to work!' he argued.

'That has nothing to do with it. He's representing the station. If you can't find somebody else, something is wrong with your management!'

And so I was relieved from duty to play in the match. Of course, this put my Flight Sergeant's nose a little out of joint but he couldn't do a thing. Orders were orders after all! I knew all the Officers and all the pilots who came to the building used to play cricket as well, so the poor flight Sergeant couldn't do a thing about it!

An unforgettable experience: I was an Associate Member of The Society of Licensed Aircraft Engineers and Technologists and I attended the 25th Anniversary Dinner of the Society held at The Guild Hall of London where I met the Duke of Edinburgh, who is the President of the Society, Prince Charles and Princess Anne.

The Cricket team Singapore 1966 - RAF Tengah
The winning team of the Far East Championship

I also had a great experience of being flown in a Lightning training aircraft organised by the pilots who used to visit the flight simulator while I was there. Travelling at nearly the speed of sound you are pushed back in your seat by the G-force. We flew over jungle, then banked and pulled out again. It was unbelievable.

After spending two and a half years in Singapore I was posted back to England in 1968 and stationed at RAF Wattisham, near Ipswich. It was while I was there that I decided to make Ipswich my home and bought my first property, a bungalow. At that time Ipswich had a small, black community. Back in the 1950's a lot of nurses were recruited from Barbados to work at the Ipswich General Hospital. There was also a lot of labour recruited from Barbados to work in the factory there, called Ransoms, which made agricultural equipment. There was also Paul's, a flour milling company, which exported flour. These organisations were the biggest employers of black labour in that part of Suffolk. As a consequence, there is a very large Barbadian community in present-day Ipswich and in fact there have been two Barbadian mayors in recent years, Albert Grant and George Hamilton-Clark. There is still a substantial black community in Ipswich, but the Barbadians have now been joined by second and third generation Jamaicans, Grenadians, Antiguans and Asians, along with the new generation of immigrants from Eastern Europe.

However, the established immigrant community only played a small part in my decision to settle there. It was mainly because I was stationed there, and could buy a good-sized bungalow for £4,500 in those days! Later I realised being in Ipswich meant I could be brought into contact with certain types of people I wouldn't normally have had access to in the anonymity of London. Through sport I was able to develop a social network with both black and white people from different levels of society. Many of my friends were directors, managers, doctors and other professionals.

After spending over two years in Singapore, life in Ipswich seemed very boring at first. After 6 o'clock in the evening the place was gloomy, no buses on the road, all curtains were drawn and I thought this was the end of the world. But, as time went by, I joined the Ipswich and Suffolk Cricket Club, started playing squash and hockey at the YMCA and things started to look a bit brighter. I got to know more people in Ipswich and eventually realised it wasn't a bad place after all. In fact, as always, I took the responsibility of making life better by being proactive, rather than expecting things to happen with no effort from me. I soon began to see the advantages of living in Ipswich. I had easy access to friends and relatives in London by rail or road, the countryside and woodland was very beautiful, and it later provided a good school for my daughter. I used to enjoy walking my Alsatian dog, Tina, in the woods in the evenings, and walking by the river on Sunday afternoons. So Ipswich well and truly became home.

§ § § § §

I spent another three years at Wattisham and eventually left the RAF in 1971 after a total of twelve years. I was asked by my Station Commander to stay on for another ten years but I had my mind on other things. The Station Commander warned me that it was 'A tough life out there.' He seemed to know what was going to happen and tried to persuade me to stay in the RAF.

Lightning MK 6 Flight Simulator at RAF Wattisham. Suffolk 1971

He told me my prospects were good and I could easily make Warrant Officer, but I was determined to go my own way. I realised that a man could get to rely on the Service because they do everything for you. You're spoon-fed and lots of people did find it difficult to adjust when they came back into civilian life. I didn't want that to happen to me. I was, after all, thirty –five years of age by then.

I'd originally signed on for nine years and it was suggested that if I signed for another three, I would qualify for a pension for twelve years' service, but it didn't happen. Eventually the Daily Mail did a story about it since it affected more than 800,000 servicemen. We are still fighting this claim.

But back in 1971 I took my £269 gratuity and prepared to leave the Air Force.

With it I bought a suit and a pair of Bally shoes.

Chapter 3

CIVILIAN LIFE CULTURE SHOCK

When I was working for EMI I went to Stuttgart to do a job for a company that had bought some digital recorders from EMI. They were impressed and asked me 'Would you like to join us?' I thought, yes, and when I heard the offer it was three times as much as I was getting at the time and I was going to have a BMW – a company car. I was going to have a flat. I'd be paid travelling expenses to return to England every two weeks. Great! So I said 'Sounds good, and so on.' The Director also said he'd like to have me aboard, as did all the engineers. I was told they'd draft the contract and let me have it in a couple of days.

I came back to England and a week passed. No contract. So I phoned them. They said 'Derrick, we're sorry.' I asked them what had happened. The EMI salesman who was based in Germany heard about my job offer and do you know what he did? He told the people back here in England. They got in touch with the director of the firm in Stuttgart and said 'Look. If you try to pinch our engineers we will stop supplying you with Digital Recorders!'

I wanted to get into sales. That was my ambition. I wanted to get into sales.

§ § § § §

My first job on arrival in Britain had been as a motor mechanic. I had done my apprenticeship with the Rootes Group, a well-known motor car firm during the 50's, 60's and into the 70's. The Hillman Imp, the Hawk Super Snipe, Sunbeam Rapier and the Hillman Minx were among their better known models. I worked in their transport and demonstration section.

In those early days I was rubbing shoulders with the rich and famous, people like Stirling Moss, Sheila Van Damm and other rally drivers. I used to prepare the cars for the Monte Carlo and other rallies around Britain. Once, I even had the opportunity to work on Winston Churchill's Humber Snipe. Sitting in the back of it filled me with awe, knowing that 'Churchill sat on this seat!' These were the highlights of working with Rootes and a sign that my stay in England wasn't going to be the ordinary experience of most West Indian immigrants.

§ § § § §

Like so many immigrants who travelled from what were then the British Colonies to work in the UK, I had come to England with the intention of staying just five years. My plan was to finish my City & Guilds examination, get my National ONC and then return home. Once I'd completed twelve years in the RAF the idea of returning to Guyana resurfaced. I went to the High Commission dressed in my RAF uniform trying to impress the people I thought I would meet. I informed the receptionist that I was about to leave the Air Force and that I was a qualified Aircraft Engineer and would like to go back to Guyana to work on aircraft. The company I had in mind was one called Art Williams, which operated a domestic fleet of planes. The woman was sitting at the reception desk doing her nails and didn't even look up but she told me she would put my name down and they would call me. She didn't specify who they were, and her insouciant manner left me a little deflated and disappointed. Needless to say, I didn't hear from the Embassy, nor did I pursue the matter further. So much for my uniform and three stripes!

In anticipation of leaving the Air Force I had already started to write applications for various jobs and so I pursued this line of intent. That was when I truly realised what the Station Commander was saying. Constantly optimistic, I completed at least thirty-six application forms and letters. After all, I was leaving the Air Force as a highly qualified specialist.

I should have been able to walk straight into BA Airlines or Rediffusion at Crawley, any of those large companies. However, even though I had visited all these companies during my time in the Air Force, I received very few replies, and even fewer interviews. Despite all of that I was still determined to leave. Eventually I managed to arrange one interview with a branch of Rediffusion at Crawley. They built simulators and in those days they were building the

Jaguar flight simulator for the Air Force. At their invitation I spent two or three days there, looking around the factory. After that, however, I didn't hear another word from them.

Out of those thirty-six applications I probably received about six replies. The place of birth section on the application forms probably hindered my progress. The companies used all sorts of excuses; I was too highly qualified for the job or, as I was told when I went to one interview in Action, London 'A lot of people in the section here would not work with you.' Few companies, it seemed were open-minded enough to take a chance on a well-qualified, black aircraft engineer. I took all this in my stride and kept going. My determination was boundless. Finally, after a few months, my persistence was rewarded when I got a positive response from Fields Aircraft Service, based at Heathrow Airport. Fields Aircraft Services were contractors who used to take people on and send them all over the world to service and repair aircraft. They had a vacancy for either an Aircraft Engineer or a Flight Simulator Engineer in Holland at Schiphol airport. I chose to apply for the latter position. The interview was with a Mr. Anderson who acknowledged straight away that I was the right man for the job but had doubts about whether I would be accepted by the Dutch because I was black. I heard nothing from them for about three weeks. I eventually telephoned Mr. Anderson, who indeed confirmed that the company did not want to employ a black man in that position. Naturally, I was disappointed but did appreciate Mr. Anderson's honesty.

Mr. Anderson did not let go of the idea that he had found the right man for the job. He told me he would still pursue my application and, as good as his word, after another three weeks I received a telegram from Mr. Anderson saying 'Come to Heathrow Airport with your overnight kit – you are going to Holland for an interview.'

When I rang Mr. Anderson to find out what had happened, it turned out that they had been trying desperately hard to fill the vacancy and they couldn't find anyone as qualified as I was. They had bought a simulator from an American company in Tulsar, which subsequently went bankrupt. Naturally, therefore, they were unable to supply any after sales service. They had a million Guilders' worth of simulator sitting there and nobody could operate it, or service the machine!

I arranged to meet a Mr. Van Rein at the BA desk at the airport in Holland for an interview. It was agreed that Mr. Van Rein would carry a newspaper under his arm so I would recognise him. When I arrived at the designated meeting place I recognised Mr. Van Rein straightaway, and went to shake his hand. It seemed a very long handshake to me and it was clear to me that Mr. Van Rein was obviously giving me the once-over. Having learned at a very early age that no matter where you went, the way you presented yourself was extremely important, I was naturally well-dressed and, with brief case in hand, gave as always a good first impression. So while Mr. Van Rein was looking me over, I simply smiled to myself.

We drove from the terminal building around the perimeter of the airport towards the flight simulator building, a distance of about four miles. I was being interviewed during the drive but Mr. Van Rein didn't ask any technical questions. He was more concerned about how I was going to adjust to working with white engineers and pilots.

There weren't any black people to be seen as we headed towards the flight simulator building and I was informed that there certainly weren't any where the Flight Simulator engineer would be based! But I had other things on my mind. I was more concerned about the technology. I was a little anxious about the fact that I had only worked on analogue simulators. The one I was about to work on was digital. I told Mr. Van Rein that before I left the Air Force I had attended Bristol University for an Analogue to Digital conversion course, but that I didn't have any practical experience.

KLM 747 Flight Simulator Schiphol Airport, Holland

It must have occurred to Mr. Van Rein at some point during the interview that he was more worried about how I would fit into an all-white environment that I was. He must have also registered my professionalism, so he was convinced that I was right for the job. Mr. Van Rein overlooked my lack of experience on digital simulators, and when we arrived at the simulator building he asked me when I could take up the position. I was delighted with the offer, but it still came as a bit of a shock. After all the negative experiences I had experienced to that point. I never thought that it was going to be that easy!

When we arrived at the flight simulator building a huge monster of a machine stood before us. Apparently it had four hundred and eighty five faults on it – nothing worked! It was the first time in my life that I had seen the front of a Boeing 747 aircraft. My mind started running; I wondered how I was going to cope, but before I had even formulated an answer Van Rein was showing me around, telling me where I was going to work and introducing me to a few people, who seemed to be quite friendly.

The Air Force allowed men who were about to leave the service a six-week period of 'resettlement.' During this time, soon-to-be-ex-servicemen were able to spend time with any company that wanted to employ them. Almost like an induction period.

I was still on resettlement leave when I was offered the position. I hadn't yet been de-mobbed. Still I told Mr. Van Rein that I could probably start the job within about two weeks.

After the interview I booked into a hotel for the night and flew back to England the next evening. On 5th July 1971 I started working in Holland, Schiphol Airport.

The first three weeks were terrible. Nothing on the simulator worked and in all honesty I didn't know where to start. Drawings for the simulator were badly done, and I had to pick my way through everything from scratch. There was nobody to help. At the end of each day's work my head thumped with strain and thinking. The whole computer rack was wired with white wires, and the white wires had gold pins in them so to stare at them constantly added eye strain.

However, as an Air Force man I was trained to start from the basics. So that's what I did and within two to three months we were down to about one hundred and fifty faults. I had to write to the States to get drawings and so on, which was quite difficult, but bit by bit I worked through the faults and got the simulator working.

§ § § § §

I fell back on my interest in sport in order to find a way to cope with the strain of work. I was living in a place called Altsmere at the time, where growers auctioned their flowers. On my way to Amsterdam one Saturday I noticed some men playing hockey and impulsively I stopped the bus, got off and went up to the clubhouse. I introduced myself to a young man there, telling him where I was from and where I worked. I also told him that I wanted to join the club and play some hockey. I was told to register with the club's secretary.

I told her I had no kit, and that I wasn't a good player, but she lent me some kit and told me to return on Sunday and have a game, which, of course, I did. From that moment on I played hockey all over Holland and Germany. As a result of joining the hockey club I was invited to play cricket by a man I met at a match one night. This man assumed that because I was a West Indian I must be able to play cricket! He wasn't wrong even though I hadn't realised that the Dutch even knew what cricket was! In Amsterdam, cricket clubs were rather exclusive. You had to be nominated by a member, or a member of your family had to belong to the club in order for you to join. But for me it was easy – I got in just like that – for being a West Indian no doubt, or maybe I was able to win people over with my charm! I was taken under the wing of the secretary of the club and, in a matter of weeks, was playing first class cricket in the first team.

At first I didn't know a word of Dutch. Most people spoke English in Holland. However, always open to new challenges, I tried to learn a sentence or so every day from the girls in my hotel. Over a period of time I picked up the language quite well. I used to spend my evenings talking with the growers who would invite me to their homes. I got to know the locals very well and they often gave me plants, flowers or bulbs. As happened in Singapore, once people got to know me, I was treated very well. I had, and took, opportunities to travel all over Holland. I was befriended by many people who gave me gifts and invited me away for weekends.

I also spent many weekends in Germany, out on yachts on the lakes and many other places. I had a wonderful time. My contract with KLM was extended from the original three months to eighteen and it included a free first class return flight every two weeks for my wife to visit. Both KLM and the people I met in Holland treated me very well. And an added bonus was that I faced no problems because of my race. I always said that someone must have been looking down and keeping a watchful eye on me.

Eventually KLM did offer me a permanent contract but I didn't like the terms they were offering. They were paying the contractors a great deal of money for my services, and after I had cleared most of the faults on the simulator within four months of being there, they asked me to train some engineers. I trained three of their engineers on the simulator. But for all that they wanted to pay me less for a permanent contract, and I would have to pay for all of the accommodation which, hitherto, was being paid for by the company. A sense of fair play meant that I turned the job down, even though I would have liked to stay.

So it all came to an end and I returned to England. Once again began the arduous task of searching for employment, writing more applications and gaining nothing but more disappointment. Once again I puzzled over the fact that I was a highly qualified person, with eighteen months experience in Holland working on the Boeing 747 simulator, but I still couldn't get a job with BA or any of the airlines. Nobody answered my applications but I pressed on nevertheless. I kept writing applications, believing that eventually somebody would answer, and eventually EMI did.

Chapter 4

AROUND THE WORLD WITH MEDICAL EQUIPMENT

I received a response from SE Labs, EMI who were now making scanners .... Brain and body computertomography (CT scans). They had just developed a new digital recorder and they wanted someone to service this equipment. I went to the interview at which I had to do a trade test. The manager said my test results were good, but that on power supplies he didn't think I was able to cope. I said 'No disrespect, but the sort of equipment that I have worked on you have never seen in your life.'

'I have been in charge of £1million worth of flight simulator equipment and you are telling me I'm weak in power supply.' I said 'I've worked on equipment that you've never even heard of and some of the equipment I've worked on in the Air Force you are never likely to see.' I said thank you very much for seeing me and I collected my travel expenses which he offered and I left. But I'd also had another interview with the same company in Hayes, Middlesex, which actually built the scanners. I went to that interview about a week later. This time the man conducting the interview conceded that I knew much more than he did. He didn't bother giving me a trade test and offered me the job straight away. One department said I wasn't good enough, another said I knew more than the top engineer. You figure it out!

§ § § § §

I had been at EMI for about eight months before I discovered, to my surprise, that the person who was in charge of the department was an ex-RAF man – he was on radar. One day he told me that from the moment I entered the office he knew that he was going to employ me. There was something about my attitude, appearance, indeed my whole countenance that told him that I was the right man for the job. Even now if I am advising young people I always tell them that appearance and attitude are very important in breaking down the barriers.

Once again my resourcefulness and commitment got me noticed and I was asked by one of the supervision engineers to do a course to service a machine which they had recently developed. They had no trained engineers to work on it. Characteristically, I wanted to be involved in any new challenge and so I agreed. I went to Camberley in Surrey, where they'd built the machine, did the course and started working on the new machine. I ran into difficulties when I met another person who had applied for the same job as service engineer but was unsuccessful. He made things difficult for me by rather churlishly withholding information from him.

But another engineer had already warned me about this man and of course, forewarned, I showed no animosity whatsoever toward him. I did what I had to do and didn't let it worry me. Eventually we began to communicate and he began to warm to me and felt able to tell me openly one day that he hadn't wanted to have anything to do with me because in his mind I'd taken his job. After that we became very good friends. After I had finished the course, circumstances conspired to transfer me to the same department in SE Labs, the location of the manager who had previously turned me down. For seven years he pretended he didn't know me, even though very few black people worked there,

Even though I was based in Ashford, Middlesex, I continued to live in Ipswich. I would travel to Ashford on Monday mornings, stay in digs during the week, and return home at weekends. Again I was in an opportune position. It so happened that the white engineers were not keen on working abroad, because of family or other reasons such as not wanting to miss Coronation Street on TV, and so one day they asked me if I would like to go to Norway to do a job. Of course, I grabbed the opportunity with both hands, and off I went. When I returned with a good report, that was it. I was sent all over the world!

The contracts would last one or two weeks. The customers were paying for my accommodation so the less time it took the cheaper it was for them. I couldn't afford to make mistakes; the equipment had to be working when

I left. During the seven years I worked at SE Labs I never had to return to a job because it wasn't completed, and the customer never had any cause to complain about me. I always tried wherever I worked, as a black person, to make sure they could never say 'This black guy was here and we're not employing another one.' I always tried to leave a good impression so as to pave the way for another black person to have an opportunity. Appearance and behaviour to me were always paramount.

§ § § § §

San Sebastian Spain

My travels with EMI took me first to Norway and following that to Belgium, Sweden, France, Germany and to San Sebastian in Spain.

Spain was an interesting trip for me. One evening I was preparing to leave my office in London when I had a call from the Sales Director. He told me that he had a problem in San Sebastian, and asked if I could help him out. He gave me a ticket, £300 spending money, and sent a car to take me to the airport. I always kept a night bag in the back of the car, and so was happy to oblige. The machine in San Sebastian had been down for nearly three months and they had lots of patients that needed to be scanned so the hospital was getting anxious. There were three engineers already working on the scanner at that time trying to find the problem so I was a little worried that I wouldn't be able to do any better.

When I arrived at Madrid Airport, I was treated like a VIP. There was a Learjet waiting to fly me to the hospital in San Sebastian. I met the doctors and all the radiographers, who looked to me as their only hope. I began work as soon as I arrived at 7.00pm. At 5.00am I was still there, and finally at 6.30am I found the fault and solved the problem. By 9.00am the machine was running and they started scanning people.

There was a young man there of about thirteen years of age. The doctors knew he had lung cancer but didn't know how big the tumour was. When they scanned him they found a tumour the size of a golf ball and were able to operate the same morning. It made me feel good that I was able to solve the problem, and possibly save someone's life. The doctor was so elated he rented a complete restaurant and they wined and dined me and all the other engineers for a whole evening. The doctor gave me his address and told me if I was ever in San Sebastian again I should look him up. I never went back, but it's a good memory to have.

One Friday afternoon during September 1978 at about 4.30pm, when I was about to leave for home for the weekend, I received a telephone call from the EMI Director of Sales saying he had an emergency. He asked me to fly out to West Berlin to look at a problem they had had on a digital recorder for some weeks. The problem was on the part of the digital recorder that recorded the pictures from the CT scanner. I'd been just about to go home and was not thinking of flying anywhere, but the Director pleaded with me and told me that he had already left airline tickets at the BA desk at Heathrow Airport, along with some travellers' cheques. The flight was booked for 5.30pm. I agreed to go. The Jaguar picked me up from the office and took me to the airport. I was met by one of the representatives in West Berlin and whisked off to the hospital.

All the engineers were waiting around for my arrival with a television crew who were featuring that particular scanner, the first in West Berlin, on a TV news programme. I got to work, testing, investigating and servicing, and eventually fixed the problem. It took less time than I had expected and, when the machine began to work, everybody cheered. The TV show was able to go out at 9.00pm as scheduled. The crew and members of the hospital staff took me and other engineers out to dinner as a way of thanking us. I stayed on for a couple of days in Berlin and decided to visit the Berlin Wall. Through all the security at Check Point Charlie I could see that everything in East Berlin looked dark and gloomy, even a little sinister. I felt as if I was constantly being watched and wondered how people could live under such difficult circumstances. However, when I returned to Berlin twenty-four years later, having seen the wall before it was taken down, the difference was amazing!

§ § § § §

Alongside my duties as a service engineer, between 1974-1979, I also trained all the scanner engineers who worked at EMI, running training courses for all those who operated the digital tape recorders. I ran two courses a year; one in April and another in December. I spent the rest of the time on customers' premises doing on the job training in hospitals. These training sessions took me all over the world, and I trained engineers who came from places as far away as Brazil, South Africa, Norway, Sweden, Denmark, Kuwait and Saudi Arabia. At that time practically every hospital around the world had a brain scanner, and consequently this was a huge business. I was based in Hayes in Middlesex and used to run training courses from airport hotels such as the Excelsior and Skyway, and also from the main factory near Wookie Hole in Wells, Somerset. I also ran week-long courses at a hotel called the George in Wells in Somerset.

The end of my career with EMI was signalled when a new man joined me on the training team. Like me he was a service engineer but wanted to be a supervisor. He was persistent and ambitions so in the end he made the grade of supervisor for the service department. However, he proved to lack the man-management skills necessary to be a successful leader and the department had more complaints from customers than they had ever had before. The higher management became aware of this and moved him into the training department with me. He was the more senior of the two of us but we were supposed to work as a team.

Unfortunately this man had a very negative disposition. It was the first time in my life that I was getting up in the morning not wanting to go to work because I couldn't stand the man's negative attitude. When I was running the courses on my own I prepared them well in advance, making course notes, booking venues, contacting the company where the trainees were coming from, finalising the number of trainees, etc. When the trainees arrived everything was organised. In this way I could anticipate any problems and fine tune arrangements.

But my team mate was the exact opposite. His method was continual crisis management. Of course, this caused a lot of conflict between the two of us. Moreover, potential students often didn't want him to teach them. Often they couldn't understand his accent and didn't attempt to cater for the fact that they were foreigners and therefore unfamiliar with some English accents. The two of us often disagreed and eventually I decided I couldn't stand this any longer. I went to see my manager and gave him my ultimatum. If they didn't move the other man from my department, I would leave the company. The management was in a difficult situation. This colleague had seventeen years' service at EMI and I only had seven. They couldn't justify firing him and, in any case, that was not what I wanted. However, they were also at a loss as to where to transfer him.

The situation went on for about a year during which time I applied for, and got, another job. I went to a place called Techmation and once everything was signed and sealed I tendered my resignation. Naturally my manager tried to talk me out of leaving and offered me more money but I had lost the thing that was most important to me, job satisfaction, so I left. EMI wrote me many letters asking me to return and, indeed, clients were still asking for me but I had made it a rule to never look back.

I worked for Techmation from 1979 to 1981, working with underwater cameras and computers to check the viscosity of oils for aircraft engines, the amount of carbon, the amount of iron, copper and so on. I used a digital recorder to take samples and work on them. During that time I travelled around the UK. Eventually the contract for this work was given to another company and I was made redundant. When I received my redundancy notice I went back to a company that had wanted me to join them a few years previously.

The company was called RTC and they were based in Watford. I started there in 1981. The company's owner was an American called Barnie Crawford. He had wanted me to join his company since my days at EMI. I used to train their engineers. The company had digital recorders in Cash and Carry centres. Orders were phoned through on telephone lines and recorded so that the workers knew each morning where orders needed to be sent. I had trained their engineers on digital recorders and when they had any major faults, they used to send for me. So Barnie Crawford knew me very well. When I told him I was looking for a job he wanted me to start immediately. He said he'd been waiting for me for the past two years!

Barnie Crawford told me to go to the Service Department, which was in Watford, and tell the supervisor that I would be starting there on Monday. Of course, when I got there, it wasn't that easy. The manager told me I had to take a trade test. I said 'I think you should phone Mr. Crawford about this.' After all, it was Barnie Crawford who had sent me. I explained that I'd worked on all the equipment before and, moreover, I had trained all the EMI engineers. Still, the supervisor didn't believe me so he phoned Barney Crawford. He received such a loud telling off from Barney Crawford that he had to hold the phone away from his ears. That did the trick and I started work at RTC.

When I arrived I noticed that RTC had about a dozen digital recorders in a cupboard that had faults on them that their engineers could not fix. I was asked to see what I could do with them. This puzzled me because all the engineers had received training. However, within a week all of the digital recorders were working! I then became the hot shot of the place. My name was on the tip of everybody's tongue as I visited customers, repaired their machines and generally imparted my philosophy; 'You should set yourself a high standard and never fall below it!' I introduced a new professionalism into the department.

I always wore a white coat and managed to get the other service engineers to wear them and to get the company to pay for them to be cleaned. This way the engineers looked proficient and they were able to keep their own clothes clean. I worked with RTC until 1982.

Ever since I'd left EMI they had been looking for me. The type of technical expertise I had on digital recording was in short supply. They couldn't get the right calibre of staff to work on them. So one afternoon, completely out of the blue, I received a telephone call from Ken White, the supervisor for the overseas services department of EMI in Hayes. Apparently someone I'd worked with in San Sebastian had been searching for me for eighteen months and he was trying to track me down because he had a project which he wanted me to work on. An appointment was arranged for me to visit them at their offices in Slough. There I sat in the office with the manager and the supervisor while they told me about a project they had in Algeria in a place called Annaba. It appeared that the hospital was just about to install a CTA 8800 Brain and Body scanner and they wanted me to go there and assist the engineer with the installations. I had always enjoyed travelling and this would be a golden opportunity. The manager joked that according to the rules and regulations they were supposed to give me another trade test. They all laughed at the absurdity of the idea! I gave a month's notice to the Crawfords and started work with EMI in May 1982.

RTC were very disappointed when I told them I was leaving. Mrs. Crawford and her husband tried to persuade me to stay, but to no avail. Had I succeeded in getting into their sales department, which was my greatest ambition, I might have considered staying.

However, the Sales Director in the company didn't think I had the potential to be a salesman. There was no doubt about my ability as a technician, but not a salesman.

I myself had no doubt that I could be a successful salesman. I was always in contact with the clients, they relied on me for technical information and trusted me. I made life easy for the sales people, all they had to do was sign on the dotted line. But the Sales Director was adamant and Barnie Crawford had to support his partner. The Crawfords were very upset and said there would always be a job there for me. It was a friendly company and enjoyable to work for, so I left the company with a heavy heart but the Crawfords and I remained great friends.

§ § § § §

When I returned to EMI in 1982 the medical side of the company had been bought by General Electric International so in actual fact I was employed by General Electric and not EMI. I took up that first assignment in Algeria in May 1982. It was the first time that I had been to an Arab country and it was a completely new and challenging experience. Algeria had just got their independence from France and the remnants of that were still visible in the form of a lot of political unrest and shortage. Food, particularly, was scarce. I overcame some of this by bringing my own food, particularly dried goods, from England but obviously this didn't solve the problem of eating generally and the shortage of food caused people to do things they would not do otherwise.

One evening I went to dinner in the hotel and noticed that the French sticks didn't look particularly fresh so, to satisfy my own mind, I decided to carry out an experiment. I took a piece of bread, initialled it DBT, and put it back into the basket. Eventually the waiter took the basket away and, sure enough, it reappeared in another basket on another table. When the waiter left, I said to the man on the other table 'If I were you I would check your bread. I think you'll find one piece has DBT on it.' The man found the bread in question and immediately left the restaurant.

I was also unimpressed by the level of hygiene in the hotel and often complained about the fact that the waiters' hands were dirty. Aware that such things caused illness, particularly in hot climates, I decided that I would have to find somewhere else to eat, and do a lot more cooking myself. Along with my Lebanese colleague, Nicholas Cham-Cham, I decided to look around and find somewhere to eat in the evenings. I also decided to take advantage of the fact that the hotel I was staying had a kitchen on every floor. In the mornings I would go into the kitchen and make my own breakfast and eventually I found a very good Lebanese restaurant beautifully located right on the sea front. The restaurant served lovely fresh lobsters and other seafood and it was there that my colleague and I ate for the remainder of the time in Algeria.

Although I didn't speak Arabic or French I got by with my friend's help. The two of us were later moved to another place called Constantine, which was about two hundred kilometres from Annaba. There we installed another scanner in another hospital. I remember that the weather was so hot there sometimes that if we left our sandwiches in the car they would simply liquefy. The heat was extremely dry and at times I did find it uncomfortable.

I stayed with General Electric for about eight years, carrying out assignments in many parts of the world. I worked in Jordan, Dubai and Iran (before the revolution) Pakistan and various parts of Europe such as Sweden, Denmark and Spain. I also lived and worked in Malta, Nigeria and Turkey.

The trip to Turkey was a memorable one. I had just arrived from Istanbul from Iran after completing a job in a hospital there. I was to travel from Istanbul to Ankara by internal airline but unfortunately the airlines were on strike. A taxi driver told me there were two ways I could get to Ankara, either by train or coach.

He suggested the coach would be better as the conditions on the trains were not very pleasant. I took his advice, not realising that it was about seven hours drive away!

The journey turned out to be quite traumatic. I was squeezed between two smokers of very strong-smelling cigarettes which was hell for a non-smoker like me. On top of that it was snowing and the roads were extremely narrow. If you looked out of the window all you could see was the sheer drop down the mountainside. On that journey I sat with everything crossed!

The passengers were so friendly and wanted to communicate with me, but no one spoke English and I didn't speak Turkish. They had to find some method of communication and the only thing they could think of was Muhammad

Ali. So they began chanting Muhammad Ali, smiling at me and chanting and clapping for the whole journey of nearly seven hours! Even when they stopped for breaks on route, they would pat me on the back and say Muhammad Ali. There was no hostility as far as I was concerned, only insensitivity. When I eventually arrived in Ankara, absolutely shattered, tired and smelling of cigarettes, I arranged for my clothes to be laundered and slept for twenty-four hours.

The representative who was supposed to meet me at the airport in Ankara came to my hotel and told me that they had been expecting me to stay at the Hilton Hotel and wait for the next flight. Of course, I had not known this, and had endured a terrible journey unnecessarily. Still, as usual, I simply put this down to experience!

In Turkey my assignment was at the Chicorobe University Hospital, Adana, which was in the southern part of the country. There I installed X-Ray systems, computer systems and scanners in the then new hospital. Turkey again offered me a new experience and I was totally absorbed by its history and, being on the south coast, I was able to visit a lot of historic sites. Friday afternoons, I would get into the car and drive along the south coast and stop to look at the sights.

On one occasion I arrived at a hotel in Marsin. I booked in, went to my room and opened the curtains to see the moon sitting on the Mediterranean Sea. It would rise at about 5.30 in the afternoon in the winter. And what was playing on the radio that day? 'Unforgettable' by Nat King Cole. I thought 'Here I am in a place like this and no-one to share it with.'

1985 I took a holiday in Antalya in the southern part of Turkey. In the hotel where I was staying I met an Austrian doctor whose name was Dr. Armgrat Geiger who worked at the Austrian School in Istanbul. She turned out to be an archaeologist. Her job was to draw pictures of broken artifacts to give an idea of how they looked in their original form. She stimulated my interest in archaeology by giving me the opportunity to visit many archaeological sites and showing me various finds. During my stay I travelled extensively throughout southern Turkey. I visited many archaeological sites along the South Coast between Antalya and Iskanderun. I visited the place where the ancient Christians used to live and keep their church, and where the Roman soldiers often attacked them. They dug a tunnel at the back of the church which ran for three miles through the mountains as a means of escape. I marveled at the places where the early Christians built their churches, in mountain caves and volcanoes, each one having its own escape route, and also at the ruins and facilities built by the Romans. General Electric helped fulfill my dream of travelling around the world.

§ § § § §

The installation of these scanners often caused great excitement among the doctors around the world, and I had quite an unexpected invitation when I installed and commissioned an ultra sound unit in a private clinic in Jordan. The ultra sound unit had various probes, which they used for removing eggs from women. At the time, women in Saudi Arabia who couldn't have children used to go to Jordan for treatment. When the ultra sound unit was commissioned, the doctor was so eager to try it out that he had a patient already lined up on the couch in his surgery. Such was his excitement that he insisted that my colleague and I come into the surgery and see the thing in action. A mixture of politeness and curiosity caused us to don white coats and masks but when we went into the surgery we were quite shocked to see this poor woman with her legs strapped in the air. When she saw us she was mortified. She went totally pale.

The doctor seemed unconcerned but we were very embarrassed and had registered the embarrassment on the woman's face as well. We left, explaining to the doctor that we really shouldn't be there!

In Jordan I joined the British Council Families' Club where they used to have Scottish dancing every Wednesday evening. I found it very energetic, particularly being a person who enjoyed sports, and I also loved to dance. They had various parties during this time. I, myself, arranged a Caribbean evening and had them all dancing on the tables! In December 1985 the clansman of the club invited me to the Burns Night Supper. The clansman said to me 'You come to our dances every Wednesday night, now you have to do something for our organisation.'

On enquiring what I could so I was told that they wanted me to give a toast to the lassies of the evening at the Burns Night Supper, and I had to wear a kilt! I thought about it and thought it would be a good idea. When I returned to England in December 1985 I told my wife we were going to spend Christmas and Boxing Day in Scotland so I could get a kilt. We went to Edinburgh and I walked into a tartan shop in George Street. I told the shop assistants that I wanted to buy a Thomas tartan. They looked at each other, very amused, a black man asking for a Scottish kilt. When I assured them that I wasn't joking, and told them I had to give a speech at a Burns Night supper, they began to take me seriously and called the manager.

The manager was very warm and welcoming. He told me that the Thomas Clan had married into the Douglas Clan, therefore they hadn't any Thomas tartan, but he advised me to use the Douglas tartan. I bowed to the manager's superior knowledge and followed his advice. The manager kitted me out from head to toe and I decided I looked very smart. I asked the price.

The manager told me this was £450 worth of tartan. By 1986 standards this was a lot of money but to my surprise the manager only charged £200, so inspired was he by my appearance in the outfit.

Resplendent in kilt

The Burns Night Supper was held at the Amra Hotel in Jordan. The place was full of VIPs; the British, Italian and American Ambassadors, General Fayed who was in charge of the King Hussein Medical Centre, Prince Rahad who was King Hussein's cousin, his wife and quite a few other members of the royal household. There were around four hundred people at this event. The costumes and jewellery were sumptuous! Sponsored by British Airways, they flew in a piper from Edinburgh, a haggis and the obligatory Scotch whisky. The haggis was piped in with style.

I found the whole ceremony delightful. I was truly impressed by the whole atmosphere of the evening. I was scheduled to do my speech after the American Ambassador. When the time came I was so nervous that my knees began to knock. I raised my head and saw the expectant faces and I was petrified but the speech went fabulously. In one section of the speech I had to do a Scottish accent which, of course, brought the whole house down with laughter. After that my nerves disappeared and the speech went swimmingly. It was a very exciting evening. I felt extremely proud that I was invited to do this and that I had managed to carry it off, more especially since I was the only black western person there, and I felt really good about it. For days after I was congratulated on my performance that night.

especially since I was the only black western person there, and I felt really good about it. For days after I was congratulated on my performance that night.

Derrick Burns Night toast

My Burns Night toast:

'Your Royal Highnesses, Honorary Chieftain, Your Excellency, Distinguished Guests, Ladies and Gentlemen.

It was indeed an honour when I was asked to give a toast to the lovely lassies among this distinguished gathering to mark the anniversary of Robert Burns.

Why? I asked myself. Because next to every man there is a beautiful and adorable lassie.

Gentlemen – Robert Burns would have been very proud of you.

Robert Burns had a patient and understanding wife who he called Bonnie Jean. Her name was Jean Armour, a woman he loved dearly.

Although some people refer to Burns as a ladies' man, he had a great respect for the female sex.

To quote one of his phrases –

Without the lassies, man seldom amounts to much in his life.

During one of his affairs with the passionate Agnes Maclehose, Burns produced a love song full of human feeling –

I'll never blame my partial fancy
Naething could resist my Nancy
But to see her was to love her
Love but her and love forever
Had we never loved sae kindly
Had we never loved sae blindly
Never met nor never parted
We had never been broken hearted.

No matter what may have been said about lassies '.....Burns gives the unanswerable retort to the menfolk in his poem.......

***Green Grow the Rushes 'O.** '*

Auld nature swears the lonely dears
Her noblest work she classes O
Her prentice hand she tried on man
And then she made the lassies O

May I ask our distinguished men and ladies to join in drinking the toast to the lassies.'

§ § § § §

From Jordan I went to Pakistan and then briefly to Malta.

In Pakistan, after fixing problems with scanners, there were £250,000 worth of spare parts left and still in the country. Somehow we had to get all this stuff out and it was an exercise in diplomacy, talking about family, drinking tea and then, after two days of this, I was finally able to explain that we needed to get the parts to the UK.

One more adventure awaited me before I left Pakistan though. When I arrived back at the hotel a Sikh man grabbed me – a total stranger – and next thing I knew I was a guest at his wedding in the hotel.

When I got back to the UK my manager told me he had been amazed that the parts had been returned as he had been trying to get them back for months.

Malta also had proved unexpectedly exciting. While I was there hijackers landed an Egyptian plane at the airport. They shot and killed two women and wounded some Americans, then threw them out of the plane.

I had been running the CT scanner at St. Luke's Hospital there and received a phone call asking me to come to the hospital immediately. I was sent there with a police escort because Americans had been involved, consultants from Germany had been flown in to see them.

General Electric trained me thoroughly during my stay with them, and I was sent on innumerable courses to their head office in the United States. In addition to this, I trained Service Engineers and Logistics managers in Northbrook Medical Centre in Illinois.

§ § § § §

My last posting for General Electric was to Nigeria in 1987 where I helped to install a Brain Scanner. One engineer was already out there.

I was stationed at Ibadan University Hospital, which was the main teaching hospital in the whole of West Africa. A lot of doctors used to leave England and other places in the world to go there and in particular to study tropical diseases. It was an extremely important hospital but because of the political situation in Nigeria, and their frequent changes of government, things deteriorated quickly.

At the height of their production, in 1974,. Nigeria had purchased the first brain and body scanner in the whole of Africa They paid nearly £1m for this machine, but lack of expertise meant that the equipment ended up underneath the hospital in boxes. When I arrived there the scanner still remained in its original packaging because the hospital room where it was to be located wasn't completed, so they were unable to install it. It had been there for three years, from 1974 to 1977.

During that time, Nigeria faced a lot of problems with their power supply, and naturally this affected the hospital. For instance, when they switched the scanner on there was no power to the theatre, so they could not operate on patients when the scanner was working. They had six emergency generators, but only one of them worked, unfortunately a normal situation, to which people had become accustomed. When the power failed, X-ray tubes and computer boards exploded.

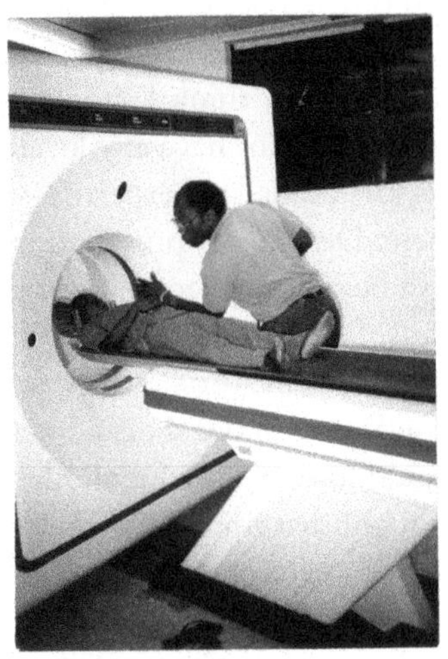

First Scanner patient, Nigeria

It was a very frustrating assignment for me, but I stayed there because, as a black man, I felt an allegiance to Nigeria. Just before Christmas 1987 my colleague was shipped back to England because of illness. Although he had been warned about the sorts of food he should eat, and the fact that he should only drink bottled water, he failed to heed advice given to him by me and others. Consequently, he ended up with severe stomach problems. The final straw came one night when I had to get up in the small hours of the morning to help him to the bathroom. He spent the whole night vomiting and had to be taken to the doctor the following day.

Because we were due to return home on leave in December, I put him on the plane back to England and finished the job in Nigeria myself. Eventually I managed to get everything working by the end of 1988.

While in Nigeria, General Electric had bought another company in France called CGR with the intention of infiltrating the French market. At the time the French had a reputation for being very protective of their industries. They rarely allowed foreign companies into their markets. Once General Electric bought the company they decided that the French, because they were already very influential in West Africa, should run their operations there and in the Middle East. The engineers on site knew nothing of this arrangement.

When I came back to England on leave in January 1989, I was called into the office and told that I was not going back to Nigeria. I was very disappointed and puzzled because the job was not yet complete. I was flown to Paris to see the man in charge and he told me that they had a lot of problems in Nigeria and he didn't think I should stay. I did not want to leave. I realised that the French did not have any loyalties to Nigeria and knew also that the Nigerian doctors needed my expertise with the scanners. I had also made a lot of friends there. Despite my protestations, they decided that I was not to return.

There was some acrimony over the fact that I was taking the side of the Nigerians. Perhaps they did not like the fact that I was a black man siding with a black nation. Anyway, they won in the end.

I was even more shocked when I was told, on my return to England, that I would have to look for another job within the UK Service Department. I had thought that since it was they who pulled me out of Nigeria, it was up to them to find me a post. After all the work I'd done in some of the most difficult places around the world, they were now telling me to find a job myself in the UK! I asked them to make me up a redundancy package. They didn't want to do this because they knew they had trained me well.

What I couldn't understand, and what I asked my superiors time and time again was – if they valued my expertise so much, why could they not find me a position in the company? The dispute went on for the three months, from January until March. I was assigned desk duty, where I sat in the office and answered telephone calls from abroad, giving technical advice over the phone. Obviously this did not suit me at all. Finally I told them either they find me a job or they had to let me go. They agreed, eventually, to give me a redundancy package and I left General Electric in March 1989. General Electric lost a very good engineer who was also popular with the clients!

§ § § § §

My real ambition was always to be a salesman, but even though I'd trained the sales people in the companies for which I worked, run the shows and demonstrations, I still couldn't become a sales engineer because that was seen as a white enclave. Sometimes I even used to get the contracts for the equipment and all the salesmen had to do was sign the sales slip because I'd already done the groundwork. But they still got all the glory, and I got no recognition. Furthermore, the salesmen usually received a higher salary, plus commission. So I used the opportunity that leaving General Electric gave me to pursue my sales ambition. I joined Allied Dunbar Financial Services.

Chapter 5

CAREER CHANGES AND NEW DIRECTIONS

Just three weeks after my return from Nigeria a London employment agency wanted me to return to the Middle East and work at the King Faisal hospital in Saudi Arabia,. I had no wish to return at that time...

As luck would have it, around the same time, my financial adviser who looked after my pension scheme, came to see me. I was between careers and he suggested that I looked into Allied Dunbar as a place of possible employment. I had never thought about going into the insurance business before, but was always sales orientated.

I had a talk with the manager of the Ipswich branch and was won over by Allied Dunbar's 'practice buy-out' scheme, which I saw as a real incentive for getting out there and doing some work. I joined Allied Dunbar. The Ipswich manager was delighted and described me as 'one of the most positive people' he had ever met.

I found the insurance business very interesting. I liked selling. I liked speaking to people, being involved with them and helping them to manage their finances. In the first year at Allied Dunbar I did very well and brought in a lot of new clients for the company. In fact I became well known for building fantastic relationships with all of my clients.

Every week the business each salesman had done was displayed in the office for all to see, and I was always somewhere near the top. This caused some jealousy amongst my colleagues. Two characters in particular who sat at desks behind me, remarked, 'We have a little high flyer here, but we've seen them come and go.' Suffice to say that of the two of them one was dismissed around four years after I joined and the other is still there and has not yet accumulated enough business for a practice buy-out. And, incidentally, has never produced more business that I did. Their desire for me to fail only served to make me determined to excel.

My top salesman prize – a formula 1 drive

Pat Maile, my PA for a number of years, said I never accepted second best, and was always a high flyer. According to her I had charisma, style and business acumen but, she said, with all his success I never 'lost that caring and sympathetic touch.' I learned a lot from Allied Dunbar. I won a lot of prizes for the sales I'd made including some trips abroad, including to Paris and Madrid.

However, I believe I did extremely well because I had a natural flair for selling, and I worked very hard.

Most of my business came from referrals of friends, family and satisfied customers. I manned exhibitions at the Barbican, Wembley Conference Centre, Ideal Home Exhibition, Barbados Expo and Jamaican Expo. My best year was when I did the Living Colour Exhibition in 1999. There I made £8,000 in commission. But around 95% of my business was done through referral. My clients trusted me enough to refer me to their friends, family and colleagues, and I was never afraid to ask satisfied customers to refer me to potential clients.

I was fortunate that Allied Dunbar were more concerned with performance than colour. Indeed, I have been extremely lucky throughout my life because many of the people I came across regarded my potential as more important than my colour. Even in the RAF I had no real problems. Of course, there were times when I had to let things go and focus clearly on my goals and what I wanted in the future.

I believe this positive attitude helped me to where I wanted to be. No matter what disappointment I faced, I just kept going.

Some of my clients were contacts from abroad, made when working with General Electric. I have created a mass of business for and from ex-patriots by showing them ways of investing offshore, buying properties and renting them and so on. I went on to spend eleven years with Allied Dunbar. When I left them in the year 2000, I sold my practice back to them, and received a very tidy sum!

However, because I had built up such a large client base, mainly through referrals, I found that my clients still insisted on seeing me, even though I had retired. I do love compliments.

I have no regrets about the career move I made, even though this did cause some upheaval in my family life. I have nothing but good things to say about Allied Dunbar. I learnt there, as I did in the Air Force, to take advantage of any training I was offered.

The insurance business has changed drastically since I joined it in 1989, so I have no regrets about retiring when I did.

Chapter 6

IT'S NOT OVER YET!

Of life and love

I realise that up to now I have focused on my career, and I confess it has been my primary concern for most of my life.

Initially, like many who came over to the UK from the Caribbean, I had thought I would return 'back home' and I was determined not to go back as the same person as when I came. I was ambitious so I did things that would help me elevate myself.

Lest you, should think I sacrificed everything to my career, I was a young man and not immune to the charms of the opposite sex, though to be honest, I'd pictured myself as living in a bachelor flat and having lots of girlfriends rather than getting married. Getting married at an early age was more or less out of the question so I did have an issue with commitment, given my ambitions to progress.

But life doesn't always turn out as we imagine when we are young.

It will seem strange to a 21st Century reader but in those days intimacy between a man and woman before marriage was much more frowned upon, though that is not to say it didn't happen. But at twenty-three it would have been unrealistic for me not to be interested in girlfriends. Most of my friends had girlfriends.

Of course, I expected to get married at some stage but not until my career reached a certain level and I could afford to bring up a family.

However, in 1958 I met Marjorie at a party. She was a good dancer and my first love. When we met it was love at first sight, but she noticed one of her nurse friends from the same hospital was also interested in me so at the party she made sure that I did not dance with that person. I think my dancing finally clinched it.

After the party we got into the habit of phoning each other and eventually I invited her for a meal. The food in the nurses' home where she was staying was horrible and I was a good cook and after that my cooking sealed the relationship.

Marjorie was from Barbados and was a nurse in a hospital in Watford. I was not only ambitious for myself, but for those who were close to me, and so I tried to encourage her to go back to school to take her G.C.E's while she was still working, so she could go higher in the nursing profession.

In those days it was far less common for a woman to pursue a career, though obviously women worked, partly out of economic necessity, but also because so many had found themselves involved in work during the Second World War and that had begun to change their expectations. But still, in the 1950's it was generally expected that a woman would leave her job when she married and became pregnant, and some employers even insisted on it. There was no equal opportunities law until the early 1970's, nor such a thing as maternity leave!

So Marjorie's priorities were not on a career. She had fallen in love with me and wanted to settle down. Eventually nature intervened and she became pregnant and our daughter Barbara was born in 1959, the same year I was called up for National Service. Obviously I had to meet this obligation and decided to go into the Air Force. But this meant that Marjorie was left to bring up our daughter alone while I was away. However, I made sure I supported my daughter financially, and any other way I could.

§ § § § §

The Air Force had developed my passion for travelling and I wanted to do lots of other things before settling down. After about a year in the Air Force I finally made the decision that I didn't want to get married. Apart from being, in my mind, far too young, the Air Force had opened up a host of possibilities for me.

My relationship with Marjorie continued only for a short while after I joined the Air Force. The end was inevitable because we both wanted different things.

I did, however, continue to support my daughter and play a significant role in her upbringing.

About three years after the break up Marjorie got married and it became harder for me to maintain my relationship with my daughter, because Marjorie's husband didn't want me to keep visiting.

When I eventually got married, two years later, I decided that I was in a good position to look after my daughter so Marjorie and I decided that I and my new wife, Sybil, would bring her up. My wife was very happy to take her.

Marjorie had six more children after that! Ironically she ended up raising them all by herself after her own marriage sadly ended. Barbara still visited her mother regularly at weekends and during the school holidays. In fact the three of us, Marjorie, Sybil and I became good friends and continued to be friends over the next forty-three years. I did all Marjorie's finances for her and her children, including arranging insurance policies and mortgages.

When I married in April 1961 it was a little surprising to me. Sybil and I married in a church in North London. Unfortunately my parents were unable to attend the wedding but they sent the traditional cakes, rum and other gifts to get the young couple off to a good start. All in all, there were about one hundred and fifty guests and some of my friends from the air Force also attended. It was a wonderful day.

Sybil was born in Guyana but grew up in Trinidad. She went to Trinidad when she was five years old, so she was more Trinidadian than Guyanese. We originally met on the TV Venezuela when we were travelling to England. We talked a lot and spent most of the time on the boat together. However, as is often the case, when we landed at Victoria we went our separate ways.

As fate would have it, two and a half years later when I went to Victoria Station to meet my sister, who had just come over to the UK, Sybil was also there to meet her nephew. That was how we met again and rekindled our relationship. It was an incredible coincidence.

Sybil was happy to raise my child from my relationship with Marjorie and we enjoyed a happy family life. Barbara went to an excellent school, St. Mary's Convent in Lowestoft. She was a boarder there for around four years and, because I was in the Air Force, I only had to pay for a third of the fees. The Air Force paid the rest.

Those early days were very happy. I had been posted to Singapore in 1966 and, eight months later, Sybil joined me there. Taking the opportunity to visit the area of her birth before travelling so far, Sybil took Barbara on a five-month cruise round the West Indies. They travelled to the Bahamas, Jamaica, Venezuela, Brazil, Guyana and Trinidad before joining me in Singapore in 1966. We spent two and a half years there, and had some great times.

When I left the Air Force in 1971 I began a career which was to take me all over the world. So, for a substantial part of our marriage, I would be abroad working. Sybil was very frustrated at the fact that when I wasn't there, nobody called. Only when I was home did the telephone ring. She would get upset because it was clear that our friends were really my friends. On my part, I was frustrated that she made little attempt to make her own friends and build up a career of her own while I was away. Sybil, too, was a nurse but she had travelled to the States in the early 1960's to do a course in hairdressing. She went on to be a Beauty Therapist for a while after the course. However, she eventually went back to nursing, having decided she didn't want the responsibility of running her own business, despite my support and encouragement.

However, I still continued the attempt to get Sybil interested in business. I had a very profitable business with a company called Amway, from which I earned nearly £1,000 per month, good money in those days. When I started working abroad I encouraged my wife to learn to drive and take over my customers. I already had a fairly extensive customer base. People phoned the orders through, so there was no need for her to do any selling. The company delivered the goods, and all she had to do was to ask the customers to come and collect them. She wasn't able to do this and refused to learn to drive. I found this very frustrating, particularly as she complained about having few friends. She obviously did not have the same head or enthusiasm for business as her husband.

Things took a turn for the worse in 1989, after I returned from Nigeria to find that the company I was working for didn't want to renew my contract. As a consequence I decided to change the direction of my career and become self-employed. I went into the insurance business. Sybil did not want me to go into that business because she thought that I was leaving a very good job to go into insurance but the way they had treated me at General Electrics was not acceptable and I wanted to do something for myself. Being an ambitious man, I thought I could do better.

My wife, however, got very upset about it and was unable to support me in my decision.

Things became strained in the Thomas household, and we stopped speaking to each other. This went on for nearly a month and, consequently, we began to drift apart. I was disappointed that my wife couldn't support me in the move I was making. I was adamant that it was up to me to decide on my career. It was no use doing a job that I didn't like. Sybil was very concerned about the uncertainty of starting a new business and clearly didn't share my zeal for it anyway. When we did begin to speak to each other again, we simply rekindled the same arguments and inevitably we split up. Sybil took the decision to end the marriage.

Realising that my wife, who was ten years my senior, would find it difficult to go back to work and support herself, I decided to buy a property for her outright in settlement. All Sybil had to do was pay the bills. Needless to say, my solicitors were totally amazed and advised against this. So, at the age of fifty-three I started all over again. I cashed in my insurance policies, paid off the mortgage on the house, bought a new property for Sybil and gave her 95% of the contents of the house we'd shared for thirty years. We remained on speaking terms, mainly because of Barbara. Ironically, when Sybil had a stroke and died in 1996, the property went straight back to me as she had not made a will.

§ § § § §

How things have changed over the course of my lifetime!

I met my current partner, Christina Carlstedt Borg, in Jordan in 1987 during one of my assignments as a trouble-shooter for General Electric. Christina was from Sweden and was working for the King Hussein Medical Society for Handicapped Children in Jordan, and we became friends. In 1995 Christina came to England to work as a physiotherapist and she found employment at the Ipswich Hospital. We met again, revived our friendship and eventually decided to live together.

My daughter Barbara, a single mother, lives very close to me in Ipswich. She has a daughter who is six, and a son, Nicholas, who is twelve years old. After working at Barclays Bank, Barbara ran a model agency. Although I was against the idea, I thought she should be allowed to make her own mistakes, and supported her all the way. Unfortunately her main sponsor went into liquidation and left her with huge debts, which are now paid off. Barbara has always asked for my advice.

Barbara has never married and has always said that the only time she would change her mind would be if she could guarantee meeting a boy like her father, such was my influence on her!

§ § § § §

Retirement? What's retirement?

Ever the business man, I have embarked on a totally new career, which encompasses all the things I've learned during a very varied life. I still know when to spot a deal and run with it, and will probably do business until the end of days.

While working in Nigeria between 1987 and 1989 I met a man named Dr. Desalu who was the Sales Representative for General Electric in New York. General Electric built the scanner that I was working on, and which I had installed in the Ibadan University Hospital. During my stay in Nigeria I had become very good friends with Dr. Desalu.

During that time Dr. Desalu approached me and asked if I would be guardian for his daughter who was about to start boarding school in England, and if I could find a good school for her in Ipswich so I could keep an eye on her. Framlingham Girls' School came immediately to mind.

Dr. Desalu's daughter, Darin, joined the school in September 1999 and during her final year there, in 2001, I was approached by the Headmistress to give a talk at the sixth formers final dinner before the exam. I was delighted to accept the opportunity.

§ § § § §

A Speaker and MC ...

I gave a talk on Persistence and Determination. I talked to two hundred girls for fifteen minutes and they found my presentation very interesting. I was congratulated by the house doctor, headmistress, and the head of house and was asked to return the following year.

Of course I agreed, as I found it very interesting to talk to young people and, of course, as usually happens with me, this led on to other talks at other functions.

So now I have added yet another dimension to my career, that of being a Master of Ceremonies.

It was while I was watching the Sports Personality of the Year on television in 1999 that I was alerted to a new path. That of being a Toastmaster.

Of course, being me, as you have gathered by now, I straightaway started to investigate; beginning with the National Association of Toastmasters who told me they ran courses. The cost of £3,000 may have been prohibitive to anyone else, but not me.

I attended the two-week course in Manchester and found it involved much more than I imagined. For example I was taught how to address Royalty, Ambassadors, people in the Military, Bishops and other church dignitaries, who takes precedence over whom in the pecking order and lots more. I had to learn the correct abbreviations of various honours, how to address people in the City of London and what colour coat to wear on particular occasions. I thought the rules and regulations were mind boggling.

Once I finished the course I set to work on getting jobs and so far it is going very well. I've hosted weddings and breakfast meetings. One particular breakfast was for Trevor Phillips when he was running for Mayor of London.

Of course, I used my contacts. For instance, I knew the Mayoress of Lewisham and am, in fact, godfather to her son. When she heard I was a Toastmaster, she contacted me.

I found I had to prepare for the unexpected. I blessed the table in the absence of the priest at a wedding, and had to ensure that divorced parents didn't sit too close to each other!

I found that being a Toastmaster required a degree of diplomacy. These are just a few of my 'appearances.'

2003: Master of Ceremonies at the 25th anniversary of the Marsha Phoenix Trust for Homeless Women, at Goldsmith Hall, London.

2004: Introduced Glenda Jackson, MP at a breakfast meeting in Lewisham in aid of the Marsha Phoenix Trust.

Toastmaster Derrick with Glenda Jackson

In 2004, I also joined the Orwell Community Choir in Ipswich. We go abroad singing every year for two weeks just before Christmas. We've been to Prague, Austria, Paris, Edinburgh and Berlin but it was on the Paris trip that a particular incident took place. We were on a trip to the Chateau Chantilly, which had been the setting for scenes in the James Bond film A View to a Kill, with Roger Moore as Bond. There was a Japanese tour group walking round the Chateau at the same time and they kept shouting 'Sydney Poitier' whenever they saw me. In the end I even had to pose for photographs. The rest of the choir were somewhat amazed by all the fuss!

2005 and 2008: I was the presenter for the West Indian Nurses Association Concert at the Westminster Central Hall, This brought back special memories for me, because at the age of twelve I used to sit with my mother and sisters next to the radio to listen to the concerts on a Sunday afternoon which came from this place.

So, to stand there over thirty years later, and address three hundred people in this Hall was a milestone for me. It was a very moving experience, which

Orwell choir in Berlin

brought tears to my eyes. And the business continues to come in. Masons' functions, charity functions and more. I'm beginning to become very well known in the field.

The London 2012 Olympic Torch Relay

Torchbearer

The London Organising Committee of the Olympic Games and Paralympic Games is proud to recognise
Le Comité d'organisation des Jeux Olympiques et Paralympiques de Londres a l'honneur de remercier

Derrick Thomas

for your unforgettable contribution as a Torchbearer in the London 2012 Olympic Torch Relay
pour sa contribution inoubliable comme porteur de la torche lors du relais de la flamme olympique de Londres 2012

Jacques Rogge
President
International Olympic Committee

Président
Comité International Olympique

Sebastian Coe KBE
Chair
London Organising Committee of the Olympic Games and Paralympic Games

Président
Comité d'organisation des Jeux Olympiques et Paralympiques de Londres

Special Olympic Torch Bearer Certificate

2008: MC at an 80th birthday celebration in New York.

Awarded the Black Staff Forum award for a motivational talk in Lewisham.

I was also MC for the Ipswich premieres of three James Bond movies.

2012: An Olympic Torch Bearer in Ipswich and also took part in the opening ceremony of the Paralympics at the Olympic Games.

My costume for Paralympics ceremony 2012

2013: MC at the House of Commons, Sweden and at a wedding in Barbados when I also gave motivational talks at four schools in Bridgetown as well as a twenty minute interview on Barbados TV. In August that year I was a volunteer at the Special Olympic Games held in Bath, UK, for people with special needs.

...and an indefatigable networker

I am also a member of Business Network International (BNI) which is an American company that exchanges business referrals. A group of people, or chapter, meet every morning at 7.00am all over the world and they finish promptly at 8.30 so that the members can get on with running their various businesses. During that time they recommend tradesmen, teachers and other professionals to each other and discuss how to develop their respective businesses. In each chapter only one profession is allowed to be represented and it can only have a maximum of forty people. If the number reaches more than forty, a new chapter has to be established. I was the Educational Co-ordinator for the group and it was my job to motivate and inspire people, and to enable them to think positively.

Barbados, inaugural meeting of BNI

Introducing BNI to Barbados

I have visited chapters all over the world, including Sweden and the USA, and have set up a chapter in Barbados. My name was mentioned in the 20th Anniversary Edition of the BNI book 'GIVERS GAIN' as the introducer to BNI in Barbados by Dr. Ivan R. Misner, the CEO of BNI in the USA. The executive directors of the chapter are Curtis and Marva Belgrave.

There are also plans to open another chapter in Grenada and other parts of the Caribbean.

§ § § § §

Things don't always work out

Just in case I've given you the idea that I have led a charmed existence, there have also been times when things haven't worked out as I'd hoped.

I had always wanted to take something back to the Caribbean and have pursued one or two ideas over the years that haven't come to fruition.

Hopefully, my book will be the start of a new trend.

§ § § § §

...and that's not quite the end

Most recently, in May 2014, I have been interviewed and been accepted for roles as an extra for advertising and TV films.

I still have ambitions and, unsurprisingly, travelling features greatly in them. My lifelong ambition now is to visit all those countries where I worked so hard to modernise hospitals around the world, bringing them the latest technology to heal the sick.

I would like to retrace my steps, Alan Whicker style, revisiting and reacquainting myself with the places where I enjoyed myself so much as an engineer, sportsman and general bon viveur. ... and on my travels I hope to use this book and my speaking abilities to encourage disadvantaged young people, wherever I may find them, to keep on going, no matter what prejudice and disadvantage they are faced with and no matter what background they are from.

And to NEVER give up on their dreams.

§ § § § §

And finally ….. Acknowledgements

I believe all this would not have come about if it weren't for two very important people in my life, and I cannot give enough thanks to them.

They were Group Captain Bater and Group Captain Davies, whom I met at RAF Melksham. These two people really paved the way for what I have achieved over the years. Group Captain Bater saw my ambition, and realised that if I got the opportunity I would certainly take advantage of it. It was Bater who gave me that most important opportunity to get into flight simulators. That was my major stepping stone.

Group Captain Davies was a disciplinarian who liked me and would often stop to chat in the evenings when he was out walking his dog and I was repairing colleague's cars.

The Captain was a very tall man, and he cut a rather strange figure walking a small poodle at the end of a long lead, but he and I used to talk for hours, much to the discomfort of the poor poodle! He was instrumental in my rise from an ordinary airman to Chief Technician within twelve years, something that was very difficult to do unless you entered the Air Force as an apprentice. I did this, not by pulling strings, but by my potential being recognised. Subsequently we became very good friends.

In addition I would like to thank my Allied Dunbar manager Graham Cook, who saw my potential and encouraged me to become a successful Financial Adviser.

I am grateful to all those unnamed people who saw the potential in me throughout my careers and made a conscious or unconscious decision to focus on the man and his worth and to either ignore or actively combat the racism that might otherwise have made my journey much more difficult.

My thanks to my editors, proof readers and friends for guiding me through the process of organising and presenting a hopefully readable book. Last, but not least, to June Hamilton who suggested I wrote it in the first place.

§ § § § §

Testimonials

Derrick was the ideal new recruit, keen to succeed and prepared to listen to advice. During his career Derrick attended numerous courses to extend his knowledge into all aspects of the Financial Services industry. He became fully qualified in his first two years to advise on all aspects of Life Assurance, Pensions and Investments.

Derrick went on to achieve a number of awards during the following years, a prestigious quality award which he received every year between 1990 and 1999. This award was only given to advisers who demonstrated a high level of retention of business through quality sales service.

In terms of production performance Derrick reached a level that only the top 20% achieved on four occasions during this period. In 1999 he became a founder member of the Zurich Franchise Network.

I left the company in 1998 but have kept in touch with Derrick on numerous occasions and his attitude to life has never changed. He is the most positive person I have ever worked with and continues to seek new challenges.

G.T. Cook (Allied Dunbar Manager)

Derrick Thomas – well, what does one say about this larger than life man that hasn't already been written and said before? I have just been a small part of his life and very proud I am to have been so.

He is a man of many parts, most importantly a very caring and generous man.

I first encountered Derrick when I went for a job as PA with an insurance company. He interviewed me and I must say I thought he was very formidable and, quite honestly, I felt somewhat intimidated. Of course, after he engaged me, I was to learn just what an efficient but also what a caring man he was.

He has risen to great heights and I am sure there is a lot more he wishes to achieve. The icing on the cake for him must surely have been his recent role of torch bearer at the 2012 Olympics. He has, course, as only Derrick can, put his experience to good use and is continuing to do so by taking the torch into schools to encourage young people to pursue sport instead of loitering around the streets and maybe the temptation to drift into drug taking.

He was a guest at the Paralympics' ceremony in London and is also involved in fire protection within the community.

I am sure there are still many things he wishes to achieve and, knowing him, I feel 'the sky is the limit.'

It has been a great privilege to have shared a very small part of his life and I wish him well.

Pat Maile, February 2013.

I have known Mr. Thomas for fifty-five years and throughout that time I have known him to be a reliable, trustworthy and loyal friend.

His personal attributes also include being calm under pressure, generous and flexible.

He has worked with me on numerous events over the years, many of them linked to the fundraising for the charity I founded, the Marsha Phoenix Memorial Trust, which supports young homeless women.

Derrick has played the role of professional toastmaster at numerous events including at the House of Lords and when I was invested with the Freedom of the Borough of Lewisham.

He has also very ably run more than one charity auction. As well as supporting the Trust Derrick is involved with a charity concerned with providing computers to his home town in Guyana, for which he raises funds and supports.

He is also involved in charity work for the Heart Foundation and is also a volunteer with his local fire service, providing advice and assistance to older people in the community and helping to protect their safety and security.

Sybil Phoenix MBE, OBE, MS
Founder, Marsha Phoenix Memorial Trust

Hold on to your dreams

..THERE'S STILL A BIG LONG ROAD AHEAD!
...KEEP RUNNIN' AN' PUNCHIN'!
NIKE
THOMAS
PARADISE
20 000
km

Natasha, pictured with Nicholas,
at her Graduation, Suffolk 1, Ipswich 2010

Derrick and grandchildren
Natasha(8) and Nicholas(12)

Derrick and daughter Barbara,
Institute of Directors
Charity Function, Ipswich

Hold on to your dreams

www.ingramcontent.com/pod-product-compliance
Ingram Content Group UK Ltd.
Pitfield, Milton Keynes, MK11 3LW, UK
UKHW020916110225
454925UK00009B/88